Wishing you blessings
always and in all ways

Praise for GARY LALONDE

"We thank you for your significant contribution to the success of our Recreational Boating Industries Conference and MBIA Annual Meeting. Your presentations to our marine business attendees were truly the highlight and brought to the program a level of energy and motivation like we have not seen in years. Comments like 'I learned something that will be very useful for me' and 'He did a great job—something I will use for a lifetime' is why I hope we have the pleasure of your company again in the future."

—Nicki Carl Polan
Director of Communications
Michigan Boating Industries

"Gary, you have touched my life and the lives of many consultants and directors in the Buffalo area. You have taught them not only to Dream Big but to Expect Big. You built their self-esteem and taught them they were worthy."

—Barbara J. Faber
National Sales Director
Mary Kay

"You consistently delivered on your promise to EMPOWER THE MINDS of over 700 attendees, both agents and managers."

—Linda Woolwine
VP Field Operations
AAA Michigan

"Gary has made it fun to come to work every day and has worked miracles with people that I thought would never change their way of thinking."

—Al Dittrich
President, Al Dittrich Olds GMC

"I would like to encourage you to have Gary Lalonde speak to your company. He is a fast evolving speaker who can greatly serve your ever-advancing team members."

—Mark Victor Hansen
Co-Author of #1 *New York Times* best-selling series *Chicken Soup for the Soul*

"Our team needed a breakthrough, and you provided a shot in the arm to many of us. We stand to be better for having attended your session.

—Larry Skinner
Department of the Army

"Thank you for the time you shared with us last week. The motivation you instilled upon our staff was phenomenal. I have received many telephone calls praising your seminar."

—Mark Pfeiffer, CHR
Director of Sales Training
Art Van Furniture

"I don't know how to tell you how much your seminar meant to me and to the participants from our Century 21 office. It was by far the most powerful group effort in which my company has participated. How refreshing to have a seminar that doesn't deal specifically with real estate technical issues or sales skills and yet is instrumental in dramatically improving attitude and increasing productivity in the offices!"

—Nanette Hebets
Broker/Owner
Century 21

"I must tell you that I was overwhelmed by your presentation personally; but, more importantly, have been so impressed by the positive impact your presentation has had on my staff."

—Gary F. Root
Chief of Police
Waterford, Michigan

"I admit that my initial purpose for attending was to evaluate your work to determine if it had value for our workforce. It didn't take long to realize that you had something very special to offer. Before the seminar concluded, I was attending as much for myself as I was to evaluate."

—Standley J. Clark
Training Coordinator
Ford Motor Company

"What I saw in your presentation was knowledge and experience of the subject, blended into a package of class participation and appropriate exercises to make your points. What I saw in you was even more important than the subject: patience, understanding, empathy, a love for what you teach and a desire to see eyes and hearts open to let your message in."

—Terry Lint
Director of Education Programs
United Auto Workers

"It has been a couple of months since we purchased your services, and I wanted you to know at this time how pleased I am and that my employees are still providing positive feedback from your seminar. It has proven to be a great investment."

—John M. Knaffla
President
PacCom Medical Billing Services

"Our staff has been exposed to numerous sales seminars over the past few years, and many have been good. However, I have never had a staff still talking about the program over a week later. This means one thing to me: you hit a very responsive chord with the staff."

—Stephen Dinkel
General Manager
KISS Radio, Kansas City

"Thanks for giving your best to our management team. Your delivery of "Maximize your Leadership Abilities" was energizing, fun and timely. With so much stress in our lives today, it was great to have a moderator that could deliver a terrific message and, at the same time, do it with humor. That takes a rare talent."

—Dianne Addington
President, CEO
T & C Federal Credit Union

"People's lives are transformed as a result of Gary's wonderful teachings. His inspiring lessons are filled with ideas, concepts and techniques for living a powerful, loving and successful life. He shares his wisdom and expertise in a unique manner that strongly and positively impacts his audiences."

—Guy L. Lynch
Senior Minister
Church of Today

"Gary pushes thinking beyond incremental improvement to the setting and attaining of stretch goals."

—A.L. Crawford
Plant Manager
Sterling Stamping Plant

THE POWER TO CHANGE

Create a Life You Will Love

GARY LALONDE

Breakthrough Publishing

The Power to Change: Create a Life You Will Love

For information, write to:

Premiere Performance Inc.
1367 Wales Center Road, Wales, MI 48027-3113
or visit our website at www.garylalonde.com.

ISBN: 0-9724010-0-8 (hardcover)
ISBN: 0-9724010-1-6 (softcover)

Editorial Coordination: Janet Boyle
and from Grace Associates, LLC,
John Patrick Grace and Jennifer Adkins

Grace Associates, LLC
PO Box 2395, Huntington, West Virginia 25724

Cover Design: Dick Allowatt
Interior Design: Jennifer Adkins
Lighthouse Photo: Tony Sweet
Pen and Ink Art: Jan Dickinson

First Edition, First Printing—January 2005
Breakthrough Publishing
4076 Beacon Hill Drive, Port Hope, Michigan 49468

Contents

Foreword

Gary Lalonde has changed my life—forever.

For the past several years I've had a nagging question that has popped into my head from time to time: "Why does it take a life-threatening illness or accident for us to appreciate life as we go along?" You know the feeling. When we have the flu, all we want to do is get well. Then, after our recovery, we typically slide back into old patterns of taking things for granted or complaining about the "small stuff."

The Power To Change gives us the tools and techniques to keep this consciousness alive. Gary has outlined a program—from soup to nuts—that helps to propel us forward on the path of making positive changes in our lives—and staying on track.

I have witnessed firsthand the phenomenal difference Gary has made in people's lives. I've seen him work these principles one-on-one and in groups of hundreds—in front of national corporations seeking to make major organizational changes, and on an individual level, helping someone to quit smoking or reduce their weight by 100 pounds.

Gary's tools and techniques are birthed out of personal experiences, and these examples are peppered throughout the book. I've found this makes such a difference in the way I relate to the material. When the message comes from the heart, as it does in this book, I just know it's genuine and will work. That's why I'm not surprised by the "staying power" I've witnessed with Gary's successes.

Whether you are going through a relationship change, a health challenge, career obstacles, or learning to speak up for yourself, *The Power To Change* will propel you on your way. Gary shows you how to tap into your inner wisdom to make the choices that are right for you.

The magical thing about Gary's plan is that it's self-sustaining. It doesn't wear off like the "glow" you feel from a motivational speaker at a weekend seminar. I've applied Gary's principles in my professional as well as personal life. I've referred him to clients, and I've been privileged to see the transformations that people have made in their lives.

Every time I talk with Gary he asks, "What can I do for you today?" or "What can I do to help you help yourself?" And he sincerely means it. I'm so grateful he has "downloaded" the information from his personal appearances, seminars and workshops into this handy reference guide that I can refer to time and again.

Whether you're going through physical pain or emotional pain (by the way, Gary points out how these are related), you'll find so many ways to heal in this book. And *The Power To Change* doesn't stop there.

Gary is not about getting you back to "neutral." He is all about coaching you to be the best person you can be. If you're "settling for less," Gary can show you how to "settle for more." As he says, "You can turn off the automatic pilot." You can gain—or regain—a zest for your life, work and relationships.

On my life's journey, I know I can always use some coaching from time to time. Think of Gary as your "life coach"—always in your corner. He has helped thousands of people break through their obstacles and come out the other side with rekindled spirits and a renewed passion for life.

Gary's principles are solid and lasting. They're universal, and they work.

If you've picked up this book to thumb through it, it is no coincidence. There are messages all around us if we just pay attention to them. You'll know if these messages are right for you.

Trust your intuition and listen to that inner voice. It's your soul speaking to you. Remember—the joy is in the journey!

In gratitude,
Linda B. Arnold
Chairman & CEO
The Arnold Agency
Charleston, West Virginia

MY BREAKTHROUGH DREAM TEAM

As you read through this book, your heart, mind and soul will open up to your true awareness that you can CHANGE, and because of this knowledge you will know you are experiencing change through a "process." My journey of change continues to manifest itself as I continue to change. I wish to thank a great number of the members of my change support team (see chapter 6) who have-played such a huge part in my changing.

—Sheryl Lalonde...my love, my life, my reason for wanting to change
—Fred Lalonde...I am proud to be your son
—Dorothy Lalonde...the world's greatest mom
—Linda Arnold...for being the Dream Team leader and my friend
—Dick Allowatt...your gift of creativity touches everyone you touch
—Janet Boyle...you took my dream and gave it form
—Dr. Anne Spencer...whose teachings continue to help me help myself
—Mark Victor Hansen...who believed in me when I could barely do so
—Jack Canfield...for teaching me that "worthy" is a worthy goal
—Bob Proctor...for touching my heart in ways that still touch me
—Val Van De Wall...for seeing in me what I was afraid to accept
—Dr. Lee Polus...your teachings continue to teach me
—Tony Robbins...you helped me reach and touch the sky
—Al Dittrich...you allowed me to teach what the teacher needed to learn
—Rick Neumeyer...may your heart be filled with the blessings you gave me
—Bill Turner...you lifted me to a height that I was afraid to look to
—Sherril Steinman...may God continue to bless you and yours with joy
—Sue Oles...you opened a door that opened thousands for me
—Sandra Kay...only you could have taught me to let go and let God
—Kathy Baker...for allowing me to know your gift of love and support

—Tammy Harper...for your direction and professionalism—great job
—David Ferensic...whose friendship is priceless
—Michael Wickett...who pointed me in the direction of my passion
—Steve Yakush...whose trust and support changed my life
—Nick Palaian...you will never know the gift you gave me—but I do!
—Carrie Stollings...you help others with a spirit of love and joy—
THANK YOU
—Bart Harris...you continue to shine in the hearts of everyone you touch
—Parry Cooper...you just keep on helping others help themselves
—Kim Morris...your beauty touches and refreshes the spirits of everyone
—Gary Peppers...you are a gentleman—thank you
—Anne Whaling...you have given me so much and never asked for anything
—John Outlaw...your humor was exactly what the doctor prescribed
—Ernie Albert...your respect and support is valued and treasured
—Barb Stimach...you are a teacher of teachers—thanks for your trust
—Dianne Addington...you inspire me
—Peter Fernandes...you have helped me so I could help others—thanks
—The thousands of participants in our learning experiences...you fill my soul with the excitement of your journey
—Each and every person who in their way contributed to the creation of THE POWER TO CHANGE

May God bless *your* journey of change with peace and joy.

Thoughtfully,
Gary

Special Thanks

As I reflect upon the list of all those who have touched my life, I think of the lady whose teachings of life's blessings, unconditional love and support have filled my soul.

Rita, we never met. We never spoke. I never read a word you wrote. Yet your teachings have not only saved my life -- they have become the basis for my life.

I know as you look down and see how your loving daughter has lived her life as a testament to your passion and zest for living and enjoying life, you know your efforts are being honored and respected.

Thank you for being my teacher through your daughter. Like you, I love Sheryl very much. I'm proud to be your son-in-law.

Gary

Introduction

What lies behind you and what lies before you
pales in comparison to what lies within you.
–Ralph Waldo Emerson

WHEN WAS THE LAST TIME you finished a book and felt that your life would change from that moment on—or that it already had changed? My mission is to help you create that kind of momentous life change.

How do I know you're looking for a change in your life? The simple fact is that most people are. I don't know anyone who is completely satisfied with his or her life. It's the human condition to want to improve our lot—whether we want more children, more money or more fulfillment from our jobs. Some of us want to be healthier, or thinner, or better-looking. Some of us are looking to meet a special man or woman.

While some of these goals may seem shallow to you, at the heart of all of them is happiness. Every person I know wants to be happy. I believe all humans want to be happy. Each one of us just has a slightly different definition of happiness.

Some people are in such constant pain that the idea of finding happiness is completely foreign to them. All they want is for their pain to subside... just a little. Sometimes the pain comes from physical ailments—cancer, arthritis, degenerative muscle diseases and hundreds more conditions. Other times the pain comes from rejection, the loss of a loved one, loneliness, poverty or guilt. This pain can be just as real and just as debilitating as the pain caused by a physical ailment.

Over the past two decades of helping people, I have learned at least a couple of interesting things. First, everyone has pain. It's true. Every single person you meet on the street, at the mall, at work or at the ballgame, is carrying a heart full of pain. Their pain might come from a medical diagnosis, the loss of a job, overwhelming debt, the illness of a loved one, the addiction of someone close to them, or estrangement from a loved one. And the degree of pain each of us carries is different—and varies throughout our life journey.

Secondly, I've learned that pain is an equal opportunity employer. Everyone, at some point in life, is going to have pain. And being rich, while it buys you lots of creature comforts, doesn't protect you from pain. Neither does love. The love of a good man or woman, a houseful of children, and friends by the dozen won't protect you from the pain that is an inevitable part of life.

The third and most important thing I've learned about pain is this: it is a gift from God.

Pain, a gift from God? It's hard to see it that way when we're crying our hearts out, or lying in bed, unable to face the day. It's hard not to believe God has abandoned us when we have to endure the suffering of someone we care about. But every person I've been privileged to help has been able to use his or her pain to achieve happiness. Their lives of searing pain became the cauldrons in which they created their dreams.

Every single one of us is worthy of getting the happiness we deserve—and every one of us can break through our pain to the happiness we seek.

Over the past two decades, I have helped thousands of people work through their pain to explore what they want out of life, and make the life changes necessary to get what they want. Every single one of us is worthy of getting the happiness we deserve—and every one of us can break through our pain to the happiness we seek. To break through this pain, we have to learn to recognize our own inner strength and understand that each of us has the power inside us to make the changes in our lives that will bring about this happiness. It's all about understanding what you already have INSIDE YOU, and understanding the incredible power of change.

People who knew me twenty-plus years ago may be surprised that someone like me has made it my life's work to help others get past their pain to lives of happiness. While I am happier than I ever dreamed I would be and I'm helping others achieve fulfillment, I used to be one of the most miserable human beings you'd ever want to know. In fact, I was very close to taking my own life. But on Easter Sunday 1987, I walked away from my hell. And what I took away with me has already helped millions of people change their lives for the better.

To understand how I have helped these people, it's important to understand how I became the person I am today. As a child, I always felt that I was "less" than everybody else. I wasn't good enough—friends, siblings, teachers and others told me so, and my grades proved it. As I grew older, I made hundreds of commitments that I failed to keep. It was painful just being alive. I left in my path a string of failed relationships, broken marriages and abandoned careers. Always failing. Always proving that what others said about me, or what I thought they were saying about me, was true. I just wasn't good enough. The pain was huge and heavy. I had no idea about the power that lived within me. I just had to escape.

I even flirted with ending my life–more than once!

Then, on Easter Sunday 1987, my life changed. I came back from the lowest point I think any person can reach—that of wanting to take his own life. What I have learned helped me change my life. This book is an exploration of everything I have learned since my lowest point. Since then, I have been privileged to work with thousands of people who are looking to break through their problems, their pain and their perceived limitations. This is the message I give to all of them:

You can have everything if you believe you can.

We can become the people we want to be. What we have to do is find a way to get past our pain, identify the best in ourselves and use our power to change. This is a task that would seem a simple thing to say. However, it is not an easy thing to do. Many people simply cannot find the best in themselves. They have been too beaten down by life, by family members and others, to be able to see any good in themselves. This book will help you find the power that I know is in you—the power to change.

You might not believe right now that you have this power. You may not even believe there is good in you. This may be the opposite of the messages you've been hearing from others and from yourself throughout your whole life. However, if you reach within yourself for patience, and make a commitment to work through the steps outlined in this book, you can achieve every good thing you have ever dreamed. You have the power!

People often say that you must try harder if you want to achieve something worthwhile. Most often, when you try harder without changing anything, you merely end up getting more of the same. We become so conditioned—so locked into what we think is right. What we do not always see is that this sets us on a cycle of achieving the same results, time after time.

One of the secrets of life is to make stepping stones out of stumbling blocks.
–Jack Penn

If your goal is to obtain a different result, trying harder is not always the best solution. Most of us have already tried harder. Some of us have done that and given up. Sometimes we end up telling ourselves, and God, that what we want is more of the same. "I'm never ever going to get in another bad relationship," we tell ourselves. And what happens? We end up in another bad relationship. We repeat this process so often that we eventually come to believe there are no other kinds of relationships. Is this the truth? No! It is an assumption we form based upon the experiences we are cultivating, whether we are aware of the fact or not.

As you live your life—even as you read this book—you will be confronted with opportunities to make changes in your life—to identify your inner power and use it to achieve happiness richer than you have ever imagined. These changes could be voluntary or involuntary, your choice or somebody else's choice. I can help you talk yourself into the success that you're worthy of.

There is a giant inside of you waiting to be released, an awesome individual with UNLIMITED POWERS. All I ask of you is no more than you would wish for yourself—unleash that giant! Move through your pain and tap into your power to unleash your true self, so that you might live your true potential. And in living a life filled with the magic you've always known to be there, you might share this greatness with others. The best part is, your power, and the great person you can become, is already inside you. It always has been!

The best part is, your power, and the great person you can become, is already inside you. It always has been!

The only barriers we have are the barriers we set for ourselves, created by the negative programming we have accepted from ourselves and from others. By first uncovering the negative programming, then setting higher goals, we unleash our mind to achieve things we would not have thought possible. I am convinced that the human central nervous system does not differentiate between illusion and reality. Once you convince your subconscious mind you can achieve a new higher goal, you WILL achieve that goal.

I will outline a series of steps to show you HOW to believe in yourself and several exercises to reinforce your WORTHINESS to do it! In doing away with the negative programming, you will gain a better understanding of your true ability and what you can accomplish.

Would you be interested in discovering more of what you're capable of? Do you think there's more inside of you? Wouldn't you like to step into the life that IS your highest potential? You already know on some level that you have the power within you to change your life. Once you realize this, and you step past all the barriers you have been conditioned to believe exist, you are on your way to achieving your full potential. You can—when you believe you can.

Life ought to be a struggle of desire toward adventures whose nobility will fertilize the soul.
–Rebecca West

My mission is to empower people to know that life is our own creation—that we are the cause, not the effect of our circumstances. In accepting personal accountability, we reclaim our power. In accepting accountability, we free ourselves from the resentment and helplessness that comes from blaming others and feeling victimized. The result is a lasting sense of certainty and self-confidence, which we bring to every area of our lives.

Thank you for giving me the opportunity to be the catalyst for your personal breakthrough. Thank you for choosing me to help you tap into your greatness, and learn firsthand the power of change.

C H A P T E R   O N E

Becoming Aware

The tree that needs two arms to span its girth began from the tiniest shoot. Yon tower, nine stories high, rose from a little mound of earth. A journey of a thousand miles began with a single step.

—Lao-Tsze, "The Way of Virtue," Sec. 64, c. 550 BC

REACHING FOR HAPPINESS. Moving beyond your pain. Recognizing the power you have inside of you. That's what it's really all about. To do this, we have to eliminate barriers we have been conditioned to believe exist. We have been bombarded over the years with messages about these barriers since we were born. "You're not as smart as your sister." "You're not good at sports." "You'll never be any good at math." "You're not as handsome as your father." "You're clumsy, careless, thoughtless." "You're a loser." "You're lazy." "Why can't you be more like your brother?"

Each of us has heard messages like these. Even the best-intentioned parents, siblings, teachers and neighbors gave us negative messages. It may still be happening! Perhaps you've made some of the same statements to your own children, grandchildren, siblings, neighbors or co-workers. These messages can cause incredible pain and create huge barriers that keep us from becoming who we want to be and achieving our true potential. These messages create blocks that keep us from getting what we want and what we deserve from life.

I've talked with literally thousands of people across the United States and Canada about what they want to achieve and the barriers that prevent them from achieving it. You might be surprised to learn that the things you want out of life are probably very similar to what thousands of other people want. Good health. Happiness. More money. More leisure time. Security. Love.

If we don't have enough of these good things, it's because there are perceived barriers that keep us from getting them. You can break through these barriers. You have the power to change.

It's really important for you to know that these barriers are not necessarily physical. These are mental—or emotional—barriers. They represent conditions or thoughts that have been planted in us a long time ago. We would like to see these barriers but, frustratingly, they don't always become clear. Just a quick example: my mother is a nutritionist with over sixty-five years in her field. Intellectually, she's close to genius, but not long ago she and I discovered a powerful barrier that was hindering her.

I used to emcee the International Medical and Dental Hypnotherapy Conference. I would ask my mother if she would come and be a speaker for us—do a half-hour segment. Every attendee got a little name badge, and speakers always had a ribbon hanging from their badge that said "Speaker." Well, my mother would not wear that badge the first year. I told her several times during the conference that wearing the badge would let other people know she was a resource for their questions, but she refused to wear it. We started into the second year with my mother being a speaker there, and again she would not wear the badge. I again kept after her to do so, but she declined. Some time later I was sitting with my mother and I said, "I need to understand the significance of your not wanting to wear the badge."

What came out, after some probing, was this. My mother's parents' income was very low, and the family went through some dire times. My grandmother made a dress for my mother out of a sugar bag but did not bleach out the printing from the sugar bag. So at school other kids made terrible fun of my mother. She experienced so much emotional pain over this that she made a silent contract with herself that she would never wear any item of clothing that had printing on it.

Who would have thought? That barrier had been implanted in her mind over sixty years earlier. Once my mother saw it, she was able to make a change, and now she has no trouble wearing a badge or even a T-shirt with printing on it.

Do you know what else? Because of my mother's teaching, I myself would not wear anything with writing on it unless it said my name, "Gary Lalonde." I wouldn't even wear the Nike swish. And of course, once I recognized the origin of the barrier, I was able to break through and overcome it.

Most of us don't actually know what our barriers are. But I can promise you this: we're all living with barriers. What we experience is the *outcome* of the barrier. And until we identify the barrier itself, and make an adjustment, we will continue to experience the negative effects the barrier has been causing. Sometimes reading something or hearing another person say something can help identify a barrier. In many cases you have to work with a therapist or at least a highly intuitive friend or relative to identify your barriers. But such work is always worth the effort. It's all part of developing our power to change.

As with all journeys of a thousand miles, obtaining the life you desire begins with one step. The first step to finding the power within you and achieving the success you deserve is **awareness**. Awareness is becoming conscious of the fact that you want to change. You also have to take it a step further and believe you are worthy of change and the success that comes with it. It doesn't matter whether you want to stop smoking, increase your productivity, lose weight, or earn a college degree. You can become the person you want to be. It is very important that you BE SPECIFIC about your goals. Understand exactly what you want. At a recent seminar I asked the participants to identify what they wanted to achieve. One man, Carl, told the group he wanted more money. I handed him a dollar and told him he had achieved his goal. I suggested he call his boss and tell him that he had achieved his goal and wouldn't be back to work. Carl immediately restated his goal: he wanted to earn enough money to educate his children, quit his job and retire comfortably with his wife. He named the amount of money it would take to accomplish these things. Now that's a specific goal.

Once you become aware of the need to change, and believe you are worthy of success, you will accomplish the goals you identify for yourself.

One young woman said she wanted a man in her life. There are lots of men. She wasn't specific about what she was asking for, so she wasn't happy with the men she attracted. She got lots of men—but none of them was the kind of man she wanted. Another woman at the seminar was very specific; she said she wanted to find an attractive, financially independent man who had values compatible with hers, get married, quit her job and have children. She said she saw herself leaving her wedding reception to fly to a tropical island on a private jet. Several of her friends at the seminar were amused by these goals, since the woman wasn't even dating anyone steadily at the time. But she was very specific. She knew just what she wanted.

I heard from her within eighteen months of the seminar. She had married a bank president's son, a kind man with a promising career. As a wedding gift, the groom's father sent them on a Hawaiian vacation on the bank's private jet. I believe this happened because the young woman had stated exactly what she wanted, in very specific terms, and *expected* it would happen—and she was not disappointed.

Are You Ready for Success?

All of us can accomplish great things, if we are ready for success. Ask yourself: "Am I ready for success?" If the answer is a resounding YES, then put your goals in writing. This will empower you and help you achieve more than you ever thought possible. I believe your Higher Power focuses on the energy you put into writing the goals and helps you begin achieving these goals. You can separate yourself from 97 percent of the population just by putting your goals in writing! Take your five most important goals, write them on a little card, and carry it in your money clip or purse. Every time you reach for money, read those goals. Keep your mind focused on these goals.

People with goals succeed because they know where they're going.
–Earl Nightingale

Accomplishing What We Dare to Dream

Years ago, when I first started sharing what I had learned with others, I wrote down a very important goal: I wanted to touch one million new minds within two years. It didn't matter that I had no idea how I was going to do it. It was important to me, so I didn't worry about the "how." I just wrote down the "what."

In the course of working with corporations and making presentations to groups, I met a man named Bill Turner, who owned a large cable television network. Bill liked my message and offered me the opportunity to produce several television programs. He invited me to Bluefield, West Virginia, where his Turner Vision was headquartered. There we produced two thirty-minute interview programs that were broadcast six times each to Turner Vision's one million subscribers.

Most people would have thought my goal was unrealistic. How was I ever going to reach one million new minds? But I believe God provided me the opportunity to reach my goal, once I decided to do it and wrote it down. Later in this book, you'll have the opportunity to write down some of your goals. Don't worry about HOW you're going to accomplish them, just focus on WHAT you want to accomplish. You'll be surprised at how successful you will be!

It's much the same with the thousands of people who attend my "learning experiences" every year. Most of these folks know they want to change their lives—but they don't believe they're capable of finding their inner power to break through the barriers that keep them from being the people they want to be. Each of us begins our journey from a different point.

I love the statement, *We're ready when we begin our journey; it's just that we know something is missing.* We realize, deep down, that there's something we ought to change—if only we could learn what that is. Usually we need a catalyst, an "a-ha!" that causes us to say, "This is my point for change." Once we experience the catalyst, we know what we have to do, and we're more likely to do it.

What would you do if you knew you could achieve more, do more, be more? What would it take for you to live up to all that you were meant to be? You can tap into everything that you're worthy and deserving of having.

Not long ago I was speaking in front of a group of agents for State Farm Insurance, providing an hour-long presentation. There was no sales pitch in it; I was just talking about releasing the power within. When we broke for lunch, a man who was an ex-football player came up to me and asked, "Do you work with people one on one?" I said, "Well, in special cases. If that's of interest to you, call me." And it was just amazing to me, because out of that group another man who had been with State Farm for two-and-a-half to three decades also came up to me and said, "I have been in a rut for the last decade. I am ready to make a change." Both of these people were ready—they just needed that catalyst.

Often when I talk to groups and individuals about change, I bring up the issue of "labels." We all carry imaginary labels around with us. The labels may say things such as attorney, business owner, author, publisher, insurance agent, speaker, trainer, husband, wife, mother, daughter, father, son. Those are good labels. But we carry others that say things such as poor, not smart, incapable, clumsy, unattractive, and so forth. Believe it or not, these negative labels can be pulled off and discarded; however, the process has to start with awareness.

You can make a point to identify whatever negative label you've been wearing, then mentally and emotionally discard it and stop carrying the burden that went with the label.

Here's a special insight: every time you take the step and try something you think you cannot do, you discover that the *you* that would not is only a *thought* that believed it could not. That is so important that I'm going to repeat it. THE *YOU* THAT WOULD NOT IS ONLY A *THOUGHT* THAT BELIEVED IT COULD NOT. I learned that from Guy Finley's powerful book *The Secret of Letting Go* (Llewellyn Publications, 1990). We have everything we need in life to accomplish everything we dare to dream. Unfortunately, so many of us are limited by the size of our dreams.

You can make a point to identify whatever negative label you've been wearing, then mentally and emotionally discard it and stop carrying the burden that went with the label.

In his book *If It's Going to Be, It's Up to Me*, Dr. Robert Schuller describes this limiting mindset with a story about a fisherman having a great afternoon at the stream. Time after time the fisherman baits his hook, casts his line and gets a bite. Each time he reels in the fish, he holds it up against a meas-

uring stick that he has cut off at the ten-inch mark. Each time the fish is larger than ten inches, the fisherman carefully unhooks the fish and throws it back into the lake. A passerby watches the fisherman throw back several big catches, while keeping all the fish that measure under ten inches, until finally he can no longer restrain himself. "I have to ask," he said. "Why are you saving the little fish and throwing back the big ones? Most people do just the opposite." The fisherman baited his hook and cast his line again before replying. "Well, all I have at home is a ten-inch frying pan."

It's that same mindset that lets us determine what income bracket we settle for, what size house we live in, what kind of car we are going to drive. If we believe we'll be at the bottom of the corporate ladder throughout our work life, guess where we're going to spend our days—at the bottom of the ladder. If we believe we'll never have the kind of house, or car, or career, or relationship that we deserve, we never will.

So ask yourself... how big is your frying pan?

My friend Barbara understands the meaning of this story. Barbara is an executive senior sales director with Mary Kay, Inc., the internationally known skin care company. Barbara told me that the highest position one can achieve at Mary Kay is national sales director. For the last decade Barbara had been one step away from this position. She knew what it took to become a national sales director, and she said she wanted to achieve it. However, in the back of her mind, she limited herself to a "second place" finish. Barbara asked me to help her achieve her goal of becoming national sales director.

As we talked about her goal, Barbara came to understand that she was keeping herself from achieving her dream because of a limiting belief system. She was always an excellent student and graduated second in her class. While that was a terrific achievement, Barbara felt finishing second meant she wasn't good enough. She got the idea that she would never be good enough to be first at anything...and she always seemed to finish whatever she tried in second place. In her head, she wanted to be number one, but she never believed in her heart that she could be number one.

Dr. Schuller's story of the ten-inch frying pan helped Barbara see that it was her expectations that led her to continue to finish second. She discovered that all she had to do was buy a bigger frying pan. This was an awakening event for Barbara. Although she was doing the steps that would allow her to be a successful professional, she was held back by the internal belief that she would always be in second place. She changed her self-perception and is now successfully programming herself to finish as a national sales director for Mary Kay.

Two ladies I worked with had multiple sclerosis, or MS, and they came to the startling realization that the MS was the glue that had been holding their marriages together. Prior to the appearance of the disease, their husbands were always away. If they weren't at work they were at sporting events or out with their buddies, and the wives had become very lonely. As a response they created, through their own minds, the symptoms of this terrible disease. The more severe the disease became, the more time the husbands spent with them. By and by both women became confined to wheelchairs. At this point the husbands, while they were not at work, spent virtually all their time with their wives.

During the workshop I offered them the opportunity to step away from their wheelchairs and resume a healthier life. Each woman made the decision that her life was better in a wheelchair than it would be otherwise.

So please know that not everyone who identifies a barrier goes ahead and makes the change. Some will look at that barrier, recognize it, then decide to keep it in place—unfortunate though I often consider their decision to be. We are people of free will, and neither I nor anyone else can impose a change upon you. You have to want it for your own purposes.

When I first started helping people achieve their goals, I found that I was good at it. I learned that God had blessed me with the gift of being able to help people find the power within themselves to break through the barriers that stood between them and what they wanted to accomplish. Soon I was in demand as a speaker and trainer, helping many people. But I wanted to be able to reach more people. I wanted to be an international speaker, trainer and author, traveling the world to show people how to achieve the success they deserve. I knew that my message could help people, but I found that I was having trouble connecting with the people who could benefit from what I had learned.

My own limiting belief system kept telling me that maybe I wasn't smart enough or good enough to reach millions of people the way my friends Mark Victor Hansen, Les Brown and Jack Canfield do. Like Barbara, I had to become aware in my heart that I have what it takes to be a recognized speaker, trainer and author. I knew that God had given me this gift; once I became aware that I had the tools I needed to share this gift, things really started happening for me. My career blossomed, and so many possibilities opened up for me. Today my message is making a difference in thousands of people's lives. I continue to attract talented people and companies into my life that help me achieve my goals.

There is no security on earth; there is only opportunity.
–Gen. Douglas MacArthur

Three of those people—Bill Turner, Jim Bazzell and Linda Arnold—I met when I was a speaker at the Church of Today in Warren, Michigan. When the minister introduced them as guests for the evening, and described their roles as major players in communications, I thought to myself, "I'm not worthy of speaking to these people. I'm not good enough."

But there came a little voice inside of me that said, "Yes, you are. And God put you here."

At the reception following my presentation, Bill Turner came up to me and said, "I want us to talk," and we exchanged business cards. That encounter led to a major contract. I was later to enjoy working with his Wisdom TV and Radio Network in Bluefield, West Virginia. And Linda Arnold has become a close friend and an important supporter of my work.

Part of the key for me was *letting go of the idea that my brain was in control of my life.* Most of us operate without giving much thought to our feelings and emotions. We believe we are great thinking machines, but it's important to remember that humans are energy, just as everything in the universe is energy. It's our thoughts that create this energy. Our thoughts are transmitted through our energy vibrations. We become magnets and attract back into our living experience the energy that we are sending out. If we think we can succeed, we will succeed. If the energy we send out says that we're second best, we will continually find ourselves fighting the number-two barrier. Barbara hoped and prayed to be number one at Mary Kay, but the energy she was shooting out kept her at number two.

We become magnets and attract back into our living experience the energy that we are sending out. If we think we can succeed, we will

As you take control of your thoughts, you can change everything that happens in your life. If you think I'm asking you to change, you're wrong. You can't ask someone else to change. Change must come from within. The little voice inside of you changes everything. The fact that you picked up this book says that you are looking for change. If you want to make changes in your life—if you want to increase your income, earn a better grade point average or be a happier person—you've come to the right place. You have the power to make these changes. You've always had it.

The Process of Change

It's interesting to consider the process of change. It doesn't just happen. Change is the product of specific processes. Take, for example, New Year's resolutions. Most of us made them last year, and most of us will find ourselves making the very same resolutions again this year. Why? Because we don't succeed at changing the things we resolve every January 1st to change. We don't meet that special someone, or lose those ten pounds, or quit smoking, or land that great job. For a New Year's resolution to succeed, for us to really bring about change in our lives, there is an important process that has to occur.

As I stated at the beginning of this chapter, the first step in the process of change is to become aware of the habit, process or state you wish to change. The last company I worked for before starting my own business was Honeywell. It was a very good company to work for, and I was very successful there. I had a good salary and a big expense account—which I used to subsidize my drinking.

Some people are surprised to learn that not every alcoholic is down on his luck and living on the street. Some can be suffering from full-blown alcoholism and still be going to work every day and leading lives that appear to be normal. But appearances can be deceiving. I carried on my drinking for years with no sense that I needed to change anything. Until one morning, waking with my usual hangover, I caught sight of myself in the bathroom mirror. I was jaundiced and bleary-eyed, with huge bags under my eyes. I looked at myself and knew instantly that I had to stop drinking.

For the first time, I became aware that I had to change my drinking. This doesn't mean that I quit at that moment, but what I experienced was the first important step in the process of change—the awareness that change was necessary. Making the decision to move past your pain is critical in achieving the goals that you write out.

I get very poignant reminders of my past every time I go into a restaurant near our house to order food for take-out. The waitress always tells me, "You'll have to go into the bar to put in your order." So I go over to the bar, sit down and place my order. Down the row sits a man who is drinking and who is perched right next to the stool where I sat for many years, bending the elbow. On the other side of him sits another man I recognize from my drinking days. Between them one stool is empty. That was *my stool.*

It always has a chilling effect on me when I see them there and see the empty stool between them. I can vividly picture myself still sitting at that bar drinking, and but for the grace of God, I would be. My life would not have become what it is now. I would not be out doing workshops and speeches on the dynamics of personal change. I'd still be there, stuck. Thank God I am not waking up every morning trying to fight off a hangover and battle through another day. Thank God I have been blessed to have people support me in my non-drinking life and help me stay with it.

We all have pictures, images and visions about what we don't want in our lives. We normally tell ourselves, no more debt, no more drinking, no more losers. I'm never going to get hurt in another relationship. Nobody is going to walk over me like this again. The interesting thing is that we're giving energy to the very thing that we DON'T want. Let's look at how we attract into our life the things that we DO want. I believe that's how we achieve success.

You have to acknowledge the need and the desire to change. Without that need, desire, and awareness of what you want to change, you will keep on going in the same old way. That is so important. Without that it doesn't matter if somebody asks you to change, if somebody begs you to change—

"If you'll just quit drinking, if you'll just spend time with me"—it has to come from within.

Life is a series of problems. Do you want to moan about them or do something to solve them?
–M. Scott Peck

You've probably met people who say to themselves, "I'm not a morning person. My life would be lots better if I could start at noon." Do you think God has assigned each of us specific times of day at which we work best? God didn't decree that you would only be effective after noon. At some point in our lives, other people influenced us, and we came to believe that we were ineffective in the morning. If you believe you can't work in the morning, or that you can't stop smoking, you're right. But if you desire to make a change, and believe that you have the power within you to make the change, you will change your life.

You need to look deep inside and ask yourself if you really have the need and the desire to make a change in your life. I believe you do. You picked up this book. There were lots of other books you could have chosen...or you didn't have to choose any book at all. Studies show that only one percent of American adults will read a non-fiction book once they graduate from high school.

That's a startling statistic, I realize, and I certainly don't want you to be on the wrong side of that percentage. Not only do I hope and pray you will read the book in your hands through to the end, but I also hope you will read many good and worthwhile books throughout your life. Books have been a major source of whatever wisdom I've been able to acquire. I am a big believer in reading books—the right books! As we move through the chapters I'll indicate a number of titles to you that have been helpful in shaping my understandings, and I'll encourage you to check them out or buy them—and then be sure that you actually read them.

Try, Try Again

Trying harder isn't necessarily what you need. Try smarter! Try something different. You have to make some adjustments if you're going to make some changes. Author Price Pritchard describes this idea powerfully in his book *You2*. He describes the life-and-death struggle of a little fly trying to escape through a windowpane. The fly's frenzied efforts offer him no hope for survival. Ironically, Pritchard says, the struggle is part of the fly's trap, because it's impossible for the fly to try hard enough to succeed at flying through the windowpane. The little insect has staked its life on reaching its goal through raw effort and determination. This fly is doomed to die upon the windowsill. Meanwhile, ten feet away is an open door. Flying five seconds would mean freedom to this small creature. With a fraction of the effort it is expending it could be free, Pritchard points out, the breakthrough possibility is there. It would be so easy.

So why doesn't the fly try another approach? Why doesn't he fly smarter? How did the fly get so locked in on the idea that this particular route offered the most promise for success? What logic is there in continuing until death to seek a breakthrough utilizing only more of the same effort? No doubt this approach makes sense to the fly, but it is an approach that will kill him.

Trying harder isn't necessarily the solution to achieving anything. It may offer no real promise for giving you what you want out of life. Sometimes, in fact, it is a big part of the problem. If you stake your hopes for a breakthrough on trying harder than ever before, you may kill your chances for success. How many times have you been told, "If you want something, work for it"? "If you're not getting what you want, try harder"? Michael Wickett, a well-known motivational speaker, has a definition of insanity; he says it's doing the same thing, in the same way, expecting different results. That fly keeps on flying into that windowpane.

I'm asking you, if you could just go back through the recesses of your mind, how many times did you start something that you were sure was going to be different? How many times was it a brand-new start, but you did the same old thing? The new people in our lives have different names, but they probably have the same personalities as the ones we left. You were so glad to be out of a bad relationship, but the new relationship is just more of the same thing. Or you were thrilled to start a new job, but you soon found the same problems you had with your last boss. By continuing to take the steps toward change, we can avoid these traps.

People are not lazy. They simply have impotent goals--that is, goals that do not inspire them.
–Anthony Robbins

So lighten up and let the power of the universe give you exactly what you want. And know it all begins with AWARENESS.

Finding Your Inner Power

Now you are aware of some aspects of your life that you want to change. They may not be as dramatic as mine were, but they are every bit as important to you—and no doubt every bit as challenging. Remember, a journey of a thousand miles begins with a single step. Today, that step is AWARENESS.

Right now, take a few minutes and think about what you wish to change in your life. Write down today's date, and five things in your life you'd like to change. Be honest with yourself as you write these goals. You don't have to show this list to anybody else, so write what you truly would like to change. Being honest with yourself will allow you to work through this program with a clear understanding of what you want to change in your life.

Please don't say "I want my husband to love me more and treat me better," or "I want my wife to be faithful." The things you want to change must be something that's going on within you. You are the only person you have control over.

As you do this exercise, consider why these five things are important to you. Take some time with this. Sign it and date it. This exercise is very important as you work towards change. Why? If you don't state clearly what you want, how will you know you have achieved it?

Date:

1. ____________________________________
2. ____________________________________
3. ____________________________________
4. ____________________________________
5. ____________________________________

____

Signature

If you wrote down some changes you'd like to make, let me congratulate you right now.

You've just done something that separates you from the masses. You've taken awareness and put it on paper. This puts you in an elite group. Only three percent of the population makes a written commitment to themselves. But I have learned, over and over again, that your brain doesn't take seriously what you wish to change UNTIL YOU PUT IT IN WRITING.

E-mail me with your goals at gary@garylalonde.com, and I will send you a Certificate of Commitment, which will represent tangible proof of your commitment.

Acknowledging the need or desire to do something new or different is the critical first step of change.

Notes:

Comment on the behaviors you now have that you would like to change:

1.
2.
3.
4.
5.

C H A P T E R T W O

Understanding Yourself

Wisdom is the principal thing. Therefore, get wisdom, and with all thy getting, get understanding.
—Proverbs

HE'S LIKE THE CARTOON CHARACTER that always has a black cloud over his head. He thinks nothing will ever go right for him. And you know—he's right. Nothing does. This person is aware that a problem exists, but he hasn't taken the next step. He hasn't examined the behavior or situation that creates his problems.

Think about what it is you want to change in your life. Do you have a problem behavior like smoking or drinking? Was there somebody you were raised with who had the same behavior? A parent, a sibling, or somebody close? I often wondered where my drinking came from. One day, when I was first starting out as a lecturer, I got my answer, but it was a little embarrassing. A company was videotaping the presentation. As I watched it later, I saw myself saying that I drank because I remembered watching an uncle who drank and who always seemed to be having a great time.

It was like a revelation for me. It had never occurred to me to wonder where my drinking came from. My parents didn't drink, but as I was talking with a group, I just blurted out the answer—I liked the way my uncle was always the life of the party. He had a great time—even if at the end of the night he might be lying under the Christmas tree, or sick in the bathroom. He was really a very sick man. And yet, I spent a big part of my life trying to be just like him. Once I understood where my drinking came from, it made my recovery so much easier.

A woman in one of my presentations at Ford Motor Company experienced a similar revelation. I was talking about the need to understand where problem behavior comes from, so I asked people to take a deep breath, and as they let out the breath, to see themselves on the screen of their imagination. I asked them to visualize the labels they saw on themselves. All of us pick up labels in our lives, from our parents, siblings, teachers, bosses, even from strangers.

The room was very quiet as people tried to see themselves and the labels they wore, but gradually everybody in the room became aware of the sound of a woman crying. First, I tried to respect her privacy and ignore her. Her crying got louder and louder, until she finally ran from the room. I quickly gave the group a break, and went looking for her. When I found her she was sobbing uncontrollably. She said, "I knew the label was on me, but I didn't know I still had all the emotions associated with the label."

The painful label she saw was one pinned on her by her mother years ago. "She told me, 'You're fat and you will always be fat.' I can remember the first time my mother said this to me," the woman said. "We were having a discussion—and in our house, a discussion consisted of one person yelling and the other person being quiet—and she said this awful thing to me. 'You're fat and you always will be.'" What the mother didn't know was that the girl's own brother had been sexually abusing this young lady, and she'd been putting on weight in hopes that he wouldn't find her attractive and so stop abusing her.

Forty years later, this woman was, for the first time, examining why she was overweight. As a result of this discovery, she sought personal coaching, and was able to remove that old "fat" label and replace it with something much healthier and more nurturing.

Before attempting to make a change in your life, it's important to understand your current situation or behavior. Why do some of you always manage to "lose" your job after you reach a certain level in the company? Why do relationships derail, even though you've told yourself that this person is "the one"? Why do some of you start fights when things get too close? Why are you unable to stop at one drink, one cookie, or one hand of poker?

Understanding ourselves isn't easy. It requires a great deal of thought, sometimes about people, situations or circumstances in our lives we'd just as soon forget. A number of years ago, again while I was still drinking, I had an experience that forced me to examine some things about my past. I was dating a woman named Kay who made me very happy. As a surprise for her I had planned a romantic getaway weekend. I showed up, unannounced, at her house after work one Friday. I told her to "pack a bag - we're going to a bed and breakfast at a beautiful little lake a few hours away." Kay told me, quietly, "No thank you."

Understanding ourselves... requires a great deal of thought, sometimes about people, situations or circumstances in our lives we'd just as soon forget.

I was stunned for a moment. Why wouldn't she want to go on this wonderful trip that I had researched and planned and booked? The experts tell us that about 70 percent of all conflict results from a breakdown in communication. I figured that I just hadn't done a good enough job of describing the beauties of the place we'd be visiting, so I started over again, and told her about the Jacuzzis and the Victorian decor and the moon on the lake. She listened to me and when I finished, just shook her head. "No thanks," she said again.

I hit the roof. I had put money down on the room, money that I wouldn't be able to get back. I had spent a lot of time and energy planning something I thought my girlfriend would enjoy, and she was rejecting it! I yelled some not very nice things at her and stormed out of the house. Kay sat there quietly, and just as I was walking out the door, she asked me, "Why do you always have to run from confrontations?" In response I just slammed the door, got in my car and roared away, too angry to think about anything but how angry I was.

A little later, after I calmed down, I started to think about what Kay had said. I had to admit to myself that she was right. I do run away from conflict. Fights don't interest me—they never have. Where did that come from? I was driving around thinking when the realization hit me with cosmic force. I'M RUNNING. I realized I had always run from conflict. The woman was a genius! I wanted to go back in and talk with her, because she had recognized something about me that I had never recognized about myself. However, I didn't want to run right back in the house. I decided she needed time to think, so I drove around for a while before going back. When I got back, Kay was gone! I never saw her again. She simply disappeared from my life.

The greater part of our happiness or misery depends on our dispositions, not on our circumstances.
–Martha Washington

That evening I began a process of self-examination. I wanted to understand when and why I had begun running from confrontation. At that point in my life I still was not the most self-aware guy you ever met, so it took me a while. I thought about it that night, and for several days later. Eventually, I became AWARE! I remembered something about my childhood that I hadn't thought about in years.

I remembered my father storming out of the house every time he and my mother argued about their not being enough money to pay the bills. As much as I've worked on going to hypnotherapists and studying books on self-esteem, some of that imprint from my childhood lingers—that programming of "We have no money," and my father's example of avoiding conflict about it. With all the dodges about money in the house where I grew up, it seems pretty obvious how I learned to handle conflict, doesn't it? But it wasn't obvious to me for a long while—not until I thought about it and genuinely tried to understand.

You can do the same thing. Take a look at the things in your life you want to change. Consider the behaviors you'd like to modify or eliminate. Do you overeat? Do you smoke? Do you gamble? Do you sabotage your relationships or your career advancement? Are you short-tempered with your spouse or children? Think about the times you have done this. Can you remember the first time the behavior started? You can get a huge clue toward understanding what's going on if you'll just examine the behavior. What need were you trying to fulfill at each point?

Maybe you started smoking to look cool. We know that about 85 percent of smokers started smoking in high school or junior high as a way to fit in—to be cool. Many of us didn't fit in with any particular group. Smoking was a quick, easy way to fit in. When you went in the restroom to smoke, you had a built-in crowd to hang around with. We start habits like smoking when we're under trauma. Examine your past to try to understand what the trauma was, and you'll be amazed at what you can learn about yourself.

Examine your past to try to understand what the trauma was, and you'll be amazed at what you can learn about yourself.

I met a young lady who had started to smoke while attending her mother's funeral. There she was, sitting in the funeral home with her cousin sitting beside her. The cousin lit up a cigarette, and the young lady said, "Give me one of those." Up to that point she had been a non-smoker. She lit up her first cigarette just as her father and her grandfather walked by. Her grandfather said, "Sherry, put that cigarette down." And the father said, "Leave her alone, she's just handling her stress." And to this day, Sherry handles her stress by, guess how? Smoking.

Have you done something similar? Do you have your own set of reasons to help justify or rationalize your current circumstances? Have you stalled your climb up the corporate ladder? Are you in a relationship that is "comfortable but not fulfilling"? Do you know what? What startles me is how many people get into a relationship in order to fill a hole of loneliness that they're in. They recognize afterwards that the relationship is not fulfilling, but since they judge that it's better than nothing, they stay in it.

Destiny is not a matter of chance, it is a matter of choice; it is not a thing to be waited for, it is a thing to be achieved.
–William Jennings Bryan

Have you limited your income to what you "need"? Most folks have! Regardless of our circumstances, we have been justifying and rationalizing them, often for years, perhaps for an entire lifetime! We make it our reality, whether it's a medical condition or disease, an unsatisfactory relationship, or a career stalled at the bottom of the corporate ladder. I have worked with so many people who didn't get past a certain level, and I have helped them to recognize that *they never achieved more because that's what they had become accustomed to.* They know how to earn $30,000 a year, so that's all they've ever earned.

There's a lot of power in understanding where you are and why you are where you are. I've come across any number of people whose income is "set" by what their parents earned before them. They're willing to make a bit more, to allow for inflation, but not very much more, as if that would somehow "dishonor" their parents.

I'm asking you to look at whatever in your life you want to change. Examine your behavior. There is a clue there. Perhaps you want to earn more money but haven't been able to because you grew up in a family whose income was limited. To ask you to double or triple that income may be too great a change for you. You need to understand WHAT you want to change and WHY you want to change it.

Now is the time for you to examine the origin of the things you'd like to change in your life.

Finding Your Inner Power

As you read, take a nice, long, slow, deep breath. Let this breath out. Take another long, deep breath. Hold this breath for five or six seconds, then blow it out through your open mouth.

Now, on the screen of your imagination, see yourself. Try to imagine how you look to other people. As you become comfortable with this picture, try to see, hear, or feel the label or labels that have been stuck on you over the years. Maybe you gave yourself these labels. Maybe your parents, grandparents or teachers did. Think about these labels. See how they have been affecting your life. Notice that you have been living your life to match these labels. (Remember how Kitty's mother told her she'd always be fat?) Did you know that more than 70 percent of people in prison today were told as youngsters they'd end up in jail if they didn't straighten up?

I've seen research that shows that people aren't born procrastinators, no more than they are born "morning people" or "afternoon people." What's been determined in regard to some procrastinators is that at an earlier time they were assigned a task with a reward attached to its accomplishment. They hurried out, got it done, brought it back, and then were criticized and told that it wasn't done well enough. There might have been a comment such as, "Darn it, if you hadn't been in such a big rush, if you'd only taken your time, the project would have come out better." So many people then just continue to take their time so something will come out better. But it never does, because they never get it done.

Aim above morality.
Be not simply good.
Be good for something.
–Henry David Thoreau

Most of us have been demonstrating our labels to the world. Now that we understand this, we can make a choice. Will you keep wearing that label, or discard it and replace it with one that builds you up? Choose a new label. On the screen of your imagination, pretend to reach up and take hold of that old, untrue label and peel it off. Fold it up—tear it up even! Pick a new label, one of good health, abundance and positive self-image. Put the new label in place of that old label.

Now, imagine yourself living your life to match this new label. Call it to mind at least ten times a day to make it a reality. You're living a life of good health, abundance and positive self-image now. Excellent. You're doing great.

Examine the reasons you developed a behavior you now find undesirable. In many cases that behavior will be the result of unsolicited learning experiences from your past.

Notes:

The behaviors I want to change originated from:

CHAPTER THREE

Desiring to Change

If we don't change, we don't grow. If we don't grow, we aren't really living.
- Gail Sheehy

PEOPLE IN RECOVERY, REGARDLESS of what they're trying to recover from, talk about the point at which they knew they had to make a change in their lives. I mentioned previously that one day I got the initial awareness that I needed to stop drinking. Eventually, I got to the point where I became sick and tired of being sick and tired. Alcohol takes a lot out of a person, and one day I just drew a line in the sand of life and decided, "I will not drink anymore."

Many people reach this point and say, "I don't care what it is going to take; I'm not going back to that behavior." Up to that point, you're spending a lot of time wishing, hoping and even praying that you don't feel as bad as you do. When you're sick and tired of being sick and tired, you're on the verge of doing something huge. It is this experience that will allow you to have the power, energy, passion and focus to do what has to be done.

Remember the habits you decided you want to change? How sick and tired are you of being sick and tired? Try to assign a percentage to how sick and tired you are. Until you understand where you are in the journey, it will be hard to proceed. Change is a journey. By assigning a percentage to how sick and tired you are, you're identifying where you are in this journey. And until you're 100 percent sick and tired of the way things are, you're probably not ready to make the change you now know you need to make.

Until you're 100 percent sick and tired of the way things are, you're probably not ready to make the change you now know you need to make.

Disease is anger taken out on the body. Let's also see clearly that the word comes from a negating of what makes our life good—"dis" + "ease." I bring this up because if one is challenged by an illness, such as alcoholism or fibromyalgia or heart trouble, then there is a condition that can be changed. When we are sick, our vibrational field is assaulted, our energies are taxed, our immune system is subject to breakdown. And illness can definitely stem from emotional stress, such as grief or disappointment.

In a state of heightened stress or anxiety, we become more vulnerable to physical problems. We actually open ourselves up to disease. Depending on what the problem is, if we keep vibrating the cause of the reduced energy, our body will manifest a disease. It's the immune system that we're talking about, a system which is constantly battling disease. When we weaken that system, then disease, which is always around us anyway, takes over.

Here's the good news, though: remember that disease is anger, and anger can be changed into something much healthier. A medical approach, moreover, is not the only possible channel for change. I support what medical practitioners are doing, but at the same time it's difficult for the medical people to get into your head and persuade you to do all the things that will bring in changes in your spirit.

I had the privilege of introducing a friend of mine named David to some lifestyle changes, courtesy of a book by Dr.

Bragg, *Atlas of Medical Remedies*. Among many natural remedies Dr. Bragg touts in his book is apple cider vinegar. Bless his heart, David was having trouble getting a good grip on his golf clubs because of the arthritis in his fingers and wrists. His game was waning and it frustrated him to see that his brother—and golfing partner—was becoming much more proficient than he was. David began to tell himself, however, that the apple cider vinegar would definitely help, and he started having a small "cocktail" of it every single day.

One day I was out on the course with David and noticed that he was really whacking the ball well. "What happened?" I asked him. "Your game seems to have taken a great leap forward."

And David said, "Well, I can grip the club now because the arthritis pain is subsiding and my hand swelling is reduced. I can grip the club, I've got better control."

A strong passion for any object will ensure success, for the desire of the end will point out the means.
–William Hazlitt

"How did you do that?" I asked

"Well, it's the apple cider vinegar," he assured me.

The change came because he could connect to something he had a passion about. And the passion was a better golf game, a better score, not letting his brother beat him. The power, the need to change, is usually associated with a perceived gain. And that perception needs to feed right into your building yourself up inside.

Start a New Conversation with Yourself

When I began to understand that I had issues with alcohol, I went to talk with an expert at work. It took him about thirty seconds to see that I had a big problem. He set me up with a counselor, who gave me an unusual assignment. She instructed me to drink every day for the next week. I said, "No problem, I've got it covered." But the catch was, she wanted me to have only two drinks each day, no more, no less. That was a problem for me. I realized that I could NOT just have two drinks a day. And with that, I had to admit that all the things I had been telling myself about my drinking were wrong. I was an alcoholic.

It became clear I needed to change the conversations I was having with myself about my drinking. I realized I had been justifying my drinking to myself for a long time. I told myself that in my line of work, as a salesman in a high-pressure job, I always had to be "on." Even if I were having a bad day, I could never let my customers or potential customers see it. I had to be charming, confident and entertaining. I had to tell myself that I was the best salesman in the company—maybe in the world.

If you've ever been in sales—which we all are, in some way—you know how important it is to believe in yourself. If you don't believe in yourself, no one else is going to believe in you, either. It doesn't matter whether your career is in sales or not; that rule is true for all of us. You're the best YOU you can BE.

Most salespeople are really selling themselves, rather than their products or services to their customers. So every day I told myself how good I was at what I was doing. The problem was that because of all the negative messages I had been hearing my whole life, I didn't really believe it. And I thought drinking gave me confidence, and took away that sick feeling in my stomach as I looked at my telephone at work every day and knew I had to make cold calls to prospective customers. Drinking let me tell myself that I was the best salesman, and gave me the courage to do my job.

What kind of feeling did the alcohol give me? Confidence! It made me feel capable—and enthusiastic. It affected my social life, too. I became more upbeat and willing to try new things. For instance, I was always convinced I was a poor dancer, and drinking made me believe I was a better dancer. If I saw myself as a poor talker, then I could be better if I drank. Also, I'd told myself I didn't laugh or smile enough before. Now I became the hearty fellow—a party boy whom everybody wanted to be around.

So I told myself that my drinking wasn't out of control. Just the opposite. I told myself that I only drank enough to be able to do my job well. That at parties and after work I only drank to relax, to unwind, to have a good time. When I began to realize that I had to change my drinking, I first had to change all the conversations I was having with myself about my drinking, my job and my life.

I believe the most effective way to stop the old conversation you're having with yourself is to start a new one. You simply drown out the old conversations by replacing them with positive new conversations.

The most effective way to stop the old conversation you're having with yourself is to start a new one.

Here's how I started. My wife asked me to attend a lecture with her. I wasn't into listening back then, but because I love my wife and want to please her, I went. The speaker was very good. He discussed dozens of ideas, but I got only one message from the one-hour lecture. The message was a big one. Here's what I learned: *You can when you believe you can.*

I wrote that phrase down—"YOU CAN WHEN YOU BELIEVE YOU CAN"—in red magic marker on an 8 ½ x 11 piece of paper and stuck it up on the refrigerator. Later on I framed it, and today it hangs in my office. Although that one sentence was all I took away from that lecture, it was enough to instill in me a desire to make a change. It has been so powerful for me because I have made this phrase part of my inner conversation.

With that small act, I had started a new form of self-talk. What's so wonderful about talking to yourself in a positive manner like this is that it can be just one or two words. It can be a sentence, a paragraph, or a picture. Starting a new conversation is the best way to start turning off the old voices. It's how I began my journey.

Find a phrase that has meaning for you the way the phrase "You can when you believe you can" still has meaning for me. Some people tell themselves, "All things are possible with God." Others remind themselves with messages like, "Just for today, I won't drink," or "I have the power to change." Find a phrase that resonates for you. It must have meaning if it is to help you. Repeat your phrase out loud at least ten times each morning and ten times each evening. Saying it out loud will get the vibrations flowing through your body and begin the process that will bring what you want from life.

It used to be a mystery to me why this works, but I now know how it works. I now know that we are all magnets, and we draw into ourselves at the frequency at which we're vibrating. So negative thoughts attract negative realities. Like the biblical statement "that which he feared came upon him," we can draw to ourselves the thing we hate or fear the most. I see the evidence in my own life, and in the lives of so many people whom I've been privileged to serve.

What you say when you talk with yourself is very important—it truly has to be POSITIVE self-talk, or you may end up with the opposite of your intentions. Have you ever noticed that parents who call, "Don't fall" to their children climbing a jungle gym are often the ones picking up the crying child who has fallen? The children whose parents call, "Be careful" don't seem to fall as often. It's because the first group of parents give their children the idea of falling—and inadvertently help bring about a fall. Try it if you don't believe me. You'll be surprised.

After attending one of my presentations, a man named Phil began a dedicated period of self-talk. However, his message was anything but positive. He was trying to balance his finances and talked to himself constantly about having no more debts—for three years he faithfully practiced self-talk. And he found that he was just as deep in debt after three years of this self-talk.

What went wrong? After a few questions, I found out that he had been asking for "no more debt." I asked him if he'd acquired any new debt since he began with the self-talk. He had not, although he was still carrying all the old debt. I explained that he could have bettered his position by asking to be *debt free.* This slight change in phrasing turned the talk from negative to positive.

Once he started focusing on being *debt free,* his whole idea about money and how to value it changed. He no longer had to feed that monster of "no more debt"—he was now feeding the positive one of being debt free, and therefore he stopped his practices of spending the way he had in his old life. Sure enough, within a few months Phil found himself debt free. He removed from his life the obstacles to getting out of debt, and he was able to live without debt for the first time in his adult life.

I worked with another man who had been the number six insurance salesman in his company. He began practicing positive self-talk, telling himself that he was the number one salesman. He wrote it on his bathroom mirror. He wrote it on his rearview and side view mirrors in the car. He wrote it on his computer monitor. He even wrote it on the ceiling above his bed so it would be the last thing he saw at night and the first thing he saw each morning. By the following year he had increased his sales by 68 percent and become the company's number one salesman. He successfully planted the message of top salesman in his subconscious, drowning out all the old negative messages. It worked for him. It can work for you!

What the mind of man can conceive and believe, it can achieve.
–Napoleon Hill

If you have a career, you need to give yourself these kinds of positive messages to help you become the best in your field. I tell myself, "I'm hot, and I'm back." This is the message I've chosen for myself, because there was a time when I wasn't.

My career at Honeywell went great for the first seven years. And, while I know that my drinking had a lot to do with my career slide, I think my expectations also had a negative impact on my career. For years, my sales manager had been telling me that salesmen's careers always went wrong in their seventh year. Sure enough, I listened to him, and my seventh year was a failure. I lost accounts I'd had for years. Everything I touched seemed to turn to ashes. Now I know it was my own inability to give myself positive messages that contributed to my difficulties at work, but at the time I was convinced that things were going wrong because they were *supposed* to go wrong that year.

There's an intriguing follow-up to this: The eighth year I roared right back into success again. Yes, my automatic pilot told me that now that the ill-fated "seventh year" was over, I "had permission" to do well once more.

It sometimes seems that intense desire creates not only its own opportunities, but its own talents.
–Eric Hoffer

I still do positive self-talk every day. Sometimes I put the messages in writing. When I left Honeywell and started Premiere Performance, the positive self-talk was especially useful. A friend who is really good with computers made me some banners that read, "Business is booming." Those of you who have ever started your own business know that most businesses don't boom right from the start. And my business wasn't booming, not at all. But I put the banners up at home, in my office and in the car. Every time I saw the banners, my subconscious mind got the message—business is booming! Pretty soon, business *was* booming. It shows us how powerful our subconscious mind is.

Listen to the Divine Talk

Ultimately you want to be able to let go of the self-talk sometimes so you can hear the Divine Talk. The Divine Talk will tell you what you need to do to succeed. It will tell you whom to ask for the order, when to make that phone call, where to concentrate your efforts, and how to bring about the success you're seeking.

Here's an example of how Divine Talk helped me. I have lived in the same home for twenty-one years and, therefore, have driven the same roads and highways nearly every day for those twenty-one years. I believe I could drive these roads blindfolded because I know them so well. One Saturday afternoon, as I was hurrying home from a speaking engagement, I heard my Divine Talk say, "Exit here." Without question, I exited the highway.

As I approached the exit ramp stop sign, I realized that I had exited from the highway one exit too soon. "What's this all about?" I asked myself. "I know better than this." I made a U turn, and entered back on to the same highway. I couldn't believe what I saw. The little gray car that had been following me had slammed into a van that was stopped in the middle of the expressway. The driver, I learned later, was killed in the accident.

Would I have been killed had I not listened to my Divine Talk? I'll never know. However, I do know that this experience taught me to pay attention to my Divine Talk. Our thoughts and words have power. This power places energy into the universe, which in turn attracts to us equal energy. I know beyond the shadow of a doubt that you eventually have to learn to shut up so you can hear the Divine Talk message. But for the here and now, practice positive self-talk. It will make such a powerful difference in your life!

Why NOW?

If you're going to make changes in your life, it's important to stay in the here and now. Remember these two answers: here and now. Here are the questions. *Where are you?* (HERE.) *What time is it?* (NOW.) Most of us spend so much time worrying about what we did yesterday or what we're going to do tomorrow that we entirely miss the here and now. I encourage you to come into the here and now. You can't change what happened yesterday or control what's going to occur tomorrow. In the here and now, you have the power to change everything.

In the here and now, you have the power to change everything.... You have the power to live the abundance you were promised.

Finding Your Inner Power

We were promised that we could have life and have it abundantly. You have the power to live the abundance you were promised. You first must decide fully that you want it and deserve it, and take the steps from there to change your behavior or situation to achieve it. You have the power to shatter your old reality. You can make your future completely different from your past. Stop fussing and fuming about the past. Come right into the here and now and start supporting yourself with the most beneficial things you can muster. Start talking to yourself in a positive manner to propel yourself to the next level.

On the ladder of life, the crowd rests on the bottom two rungs. There's no crowd at the top. Here's a message one of my mentors gave me, and I have held it close to my heart ever since. He told me, *"Success wants you more than you want it!"* If you believe that success is waiting for you and wanting you, you literally can talk yourself to the top—visualize your way to success beyond your imagination.

How powerful your mind is! If you could see yourself as being happier, more successful, wealthier and healthier, you *would be* happier, more successful, wealthier and healthier. You have the power. If you're not picturing yourself achieving your goals, you're wasting the power you possess.

You say you want to travel. Most of us travel every day...from home to work and back again. You probably mean you want to go to a tropical island or the beautiful cities of Europe. Know what you want. State your goals specifically. Write one of your personal goals on each of five index cards, and put them in prominent places throughout your house, car and office. Focus on that goal every time you see one of these cards.

Give your goals the right to live within the written word, then live within your mind's eye... and you will soon find them living truly within your life. You have the power to achieve all your dreams! Define those dreams as *realities living within your life*, and those dreams become realities.

And now for a tip about an incredible "sleeper" book—something that will help you seize the moment, name and demolish your fears, and soar into a mode of "can do and will do." It's called *The Knight in Rusty Armor*, and it was written by Robert Fisher, a talented radio, TV and motion-picture scriptwriter. Fisher sets his fable back in the days of medieval knights, Merlin the Magician, and castles to be conquered. It's a quick but life-changing read. You will enjoy putting yourself in the place of the book's knight-hero as he launches forth through Merlin's woods, through a series of challenging castles, and on to the "summit of truth."

You can order this book from Amazon.com, through your local bookstore, or directly from the Wilshire Book Company, 12015 Sherman Road, North Hollywood, CA 91605. The publisher's web address is www.mpowers.com. I have made this book available through my website: www.garylalonde.com.

What are you sick and tired of?
Experience being sick and tired of the behaviors you want to change.

____

____

____

____

____

____

____

____

____

____

____

____

____

C H A P T E R   F O U R

Loving the Inner You

You, yourself, as much as anybody in the entire universe, deserve your love and affection.
—Buddha

THE FOURTH STEP AS YOU FIND your inner power consists of just two words: Lighten up. That's easy to say, but much more difficult to accomplish. By this time, if you're working the steps with me, you're aware of the change you want to make in your life and you understand where your problem behavior or situation originated. You want to change. Now it's time for Step Four. It's time to show yourself some kindness. For the majority of us, this is the most difficult step of all. We find it much easier to love others than to love ourselves.

What a man thinks of himself...determines, or rather indicates, his fate.
–Henry David Thoreau

Think of the conversations you had with yourself this morning. You looked in the mirror and perhaps you thought about how you hated your haircut, how old you looked, how unattractive you found yourself. Perhaps you told yourself you hated your clothes, your weight or just a blanket of "everything" about yourself. Wouldn't it be great if you could change the way you felt about yourself? You can do it, and you can begin immediately just by showing yourself a little kindness.

To fall in love with yourself is the first secret of happiness. Then if you're not a good mixer you can always fall back on your own company.
–Robert Morley

I encourage you to start your mornings the way I do. Get out of bed in the morning, walk into the bathroom, look in the mirror, and tell yourself, *"I am hot and I am back."* Tell yourself, *"I love and approve of myself,"* and *"I am worthy NOW."*

Positive, Loving Self-Talk

We talk to ourselves all the time. Most of us tell ourselves some variation of the negative messages we have heard all our lives. We are just repeating the messages that have caused us so much pain, and contributed to the negative way we view ourselves. What a difference we could make in our lives if we could make the talk positive and useful. Just as we learned to use self-talk as a motivational tool in Chapter 3, we can also use positive self-talk to learn to love ourselves.

Here are three phrases that I suggest you start with, no matter what behavior you want to change. Take this message into your heart and let it sing within you:

1. I love and approve of myself.

2. I am happy, healthy, safe and successful.

3. I am worthy NOW.

I can remember the tears that came down my face as I said these out loud for the first time. Some people will be able to say them with no problem. Other people will find them almost impossible to say, and even harder to believe, as I did. For people of notably low self-esteem, which was my case, it's important to say these faithfully every day, and say them out loud.

This is the healthiest way to start a new conversation with yourself. If you're self-conscious, you don't have to practice them in front of anyone else. No one but you needs to hear these words. Once you begin to believe them, you will have begun to find the power to change.

When I started positive self-talk I was embarrassed to be doing it, and especially embarrassed to be seen doing it. If someone in the car next to me happened to glance my way while I was practicing positive self-talk, I'd shut up immediately. It didn't matter that I had never seen the person before, and would most likely never see him again. I worried about what he might think of me. I didn't understand yet that what really matters is what *I* think of me.

We all spend so much time trying to please everybody else around us. You will drive yourself mad trying to please everyone around you. The honest truth is that other people are so absorbed in their own issues, they probably don't notice us at all.

So I'm asking you to do something you might think is silly. Start talking to yourself. Do it over and over. When I started doing this, I thought that ten times in the morning and ten times in the evening would make a big difference in my life. But then I realized that if ten times in the morning was good, fifty was better. Repeat the phrases as many times as it takes each day until you believe them. The more you repeat them the tighter your circle of thought becomes. Eventually the thought becomes reality. It becomes impossible to separate the thought that you're healthy, happy and successful, from the you that *is* happy, healthy and successful.

It becomes impossible to separate the thought that you're healthy, happy and successful, from the you that is *happy, healthy and successful.*

I worked with a young lady who at the age of fifteen got pregnant. Back then parents shipped their daughters away to shield them from neighbors. The mother went with her daughter the day of delivery. The delivery produced two children. The stunned mother, looking at her daughter, said, "Now look what you've done. No man is ever going to want you." And this daughter ended up living her life with men who used her but did not respect or want her.

So what we speak out about ourselves or others, we attract. The negative words spoken about us by others or by ourselves become self-fulfilling prophesies. On the other hand, if the thoughts you are projecting about yourself are positive—if you get up in the morning and say to yourself, convincingly, "It's a beautiful day and I am going to have success on this day"—that becomes your reality.

How do we know that self-talk works? One way we know is by looking at the impact that others' words have on us. Most of us believe everything that adults told us when we were children. Those of you who are parents should be aware that your words have an incredibly important effect on your children.

In his book *What to Say When You Talk to Yourself*, Shad Helmstetter tells the story of a man who wanted nothing more as a child than to play in the school marching band. He waited for years until he was old enough to try out for the band. The band director handed him a trumpet, which he had never before held in his hands, and told him to play it. The boy did the best he could but couldn't produce very pleasant sounds. He had never had a lesson, but he tried his best. He figured that if he could just make the band, he could take the horn home and practice all the time.

After the tryouts, he was waiting in the hall for the results and overheard the band director tell his teacher, "That boy was terrible. He will never be able to play a musical instrument." What a devastating blow for a child! Not only did he not make the marching band, but he learned that day that he would NEVER be able to play a musical instrument. Those careless words had such an impact on him. He did not try to learn to play an instrument—because he believed that he would never be able to do it.

Finally, after many years had passed, he rented a piano, and now, when nobody else is around, he has gotten the courage to try to learn to play the piano on his own. It took him years to gather the courage to even try. By learning to play the piano, the man says, he has learned that his band director was WRONG! "Worse yet, I believed him," he said.

A woman I knew always wanted to learn to dance, but never thought she would be able to. In the restroom at a junior high school dance, she had overheard someone she considered her friend say, "Judy is a good dancer, and Noreen is a pretty good dancer, but Karen is just embarrassing out there." Karen was devastated. She felt clumsy and uncoordinated. From that moment she lost the courage to even try dancing...even when a boy she secretly liked asked her to dance. She avoided dances and proms in high school, and would only dance slow dances when she absolutely couldn't get out of it.

Our doubts are traitors, and make us lose the good we oft might win, by fearing to attempt.
–William Shakespeare

Finally, as an adult she got the courage to take an adult dance class as part of a rehabilitation program after a car accident. Karen was stunned to find that she wasn't uncoordinated at all. In a room lined with mirrors, she watched as she moved to the music. She was able to follow the beat. She could do the steps the instructor demonstrated. In the mirror Karen saw herself the way she really was—a woman moving gracefully, rhythmically to the music. She felt the music inside her, and danced as if she had been doing it all her life.

Karen finished the dance class and signed up for another and another. Today she continues to dance, both in classes and for personal enjoyment at weddings and parties with her husband and anyone else who asks her. Karen's only regret is that she missed so much fun over the years.

Who got into your head and told you that you couldn't do something? Who said that you were too old, too young, too stupid or too clumsy to do what you want to do? Who lied to you? Maybe they lied for what they thought were good reasons... maybe they thought they were protecting you or keeping you from making what they saw as a big mistake. But the fact is, they lied to you and told you that you could not do it. Today you still hear that voice in your head.

Children between birth and the age of seven or eight are little sponges. Their reasoning powers are not developed yet, and so the messages they hear are very powerful. And these messages work both ways. I remember some very positive messages I got when I was a young child, and they stayed with me all my life.

My grandparents lived out in the country, and when they'd come to visit us on weekends they'd bring produce from their farm, which I began selling to our neighbors. I wanted a wagon to make it easier to deliver the produce, and my grandmother became my partner in the produce business. She financed my wagon, and every week I paid her 90 percent of what I got from the neighbors until the wagon was paid off.

Accept the good that is within you. Look at what you do well and praise yourself for it! You are worthy of this praise, just as you are worthy of whatever good things you wish for yourself.

Some people have criticized Grandma for charging me, but I learned some important lessons. I learned that the things you want—desire—are worth working for, and that I had the ability to fulfill my commitments. I also learned that I was a very good salesman. The neighbors and my parents and grandparents started calling me the little salesman. They told me I was such a good salesman that I could sell ice to Eskimos. I heard this message, I believed it, and it served me well throughout my life. How do you think I became so successful at Honeywell? It was because I knew I could sell anything to anyone.

I was fortunate. I got this very positive message, along with some negative ones. Many of us get no positive messages, and we spend our lives in pain, believing that we are no good. There is good in all of us. There is power in all of us. Accept the good that is within you.

Look at what you do well and praise yourself for it! You are worthy of this praise, just as you are worthy of whatever good things you wish for yourself. Do you want to earn more money? You're worth it. Change your life so you can make more money. Do you want to get back to the same clothing size you wore at your wedding? You're worth it. You have to want to change and then believe you can change. Change your self-talk to the POSITIVE.

At home tonight, look in the mirror and really see yourself. Write the word "worthy" on the mirror with soap. Tell yourself over and over again that you ARE worthy. Then write one of your specific goals on your mirror as a daily reminder of your goal.

Unplugging the Automatic Pilot

Most people coast through their jobs—indeed, their very lives–on automatic pilot. They have no passion, no zest for what they're doing. They're like the old bumper stickers, "I owe, I owe, so off to work I go." It's as though they're walking through life wearing a big "kick me" sign on their back. This sign tells the universe, "OK life, give it to me." They don't take an active part in bringing good things into their lives, and they're all too willing to take whatever happens to come their way.

You can turn off the automatic pilot. You can regain some of the passion you used to have for your life, work and relationships. You can do this simply by starting to show yourself some kindness. When you start this process it may be difficult. Begin by praising yourself. "I am really good at my job." "I'm the best I can be." "I'm a great father."

When you start talking like this, your spouse, partner, roommate or office mate may think you're crazy, but keep at it. All of us need to receive kind words. Compliments are really important. But most of us are stingy in the compliments we give. Consequently, we're not very accustomed to getting compliments. In one month, how many compliments do we receive? On the average, studies show that each of us gets one compliment—in a whole month! That is not enough to help us thrive.

Work on showing yourself, and the people around you, some kindness every day. Give five compliments, or more, each day and a funny thing will begin to happen. Although you're giving the compliments to someone else, you are the one who will benefit most. Let me explain.

The human brain is a very powerful organ. Although it weighs only about three pounds, it is made up of some eighteen billion to thirty billion nerve cells. Our brains are divided into two parts: the conscious part that is reading and understanding these words, and the subconscious part that operates below the conscious mind. The conscious mind acts like the water filter on your tap or the air filter on your furnace. It filters all the information that comes to you. The conscious mind filters all incoming information through beliefs and values that we believe are our own, but have been formed by our parents, teachers and others to whom we were exposed.

For some people, this is a tragic fact because many of our teachers, parents and others provided us with faulty information and created the negative barriers. The subconscious mind does not reason nor judge; it has no sense of humor. It is the body's computer system. When you press the "enter" button, whatever file you opened in your subconscious mind saves exactly what was input.

There are files in your mind for every experience you ever had. Every time you felt love, happiness or sadness, these emotions were filed away in a file folder based on the subject. When we lapse into our old negative way of thinking and start criticizing or condemning someone, our subconscious mind assumes that it is a conversation about ourselves. It attacks an area of our self-image and self-confidence, as if the thoughts were truly about us. We cannot afford the luxury of a negative thought or emotion about another person because it is filed as a thought about ourselves.

These thoughts constantly vibrate inside us. Just as our radios pick up different transmissions from dozens of stations, our bodies tune in to the feelings and emotions floating through the universe. When we send out negative thoughts, they attach to negative energies in the universe and return to us. We can end up creating the very thing we fear in our life. On the other hand, when we send out positive feelings and emotions, we tend to find positive, supportive people around us.

This is a huge lesson for us. Remember Barbara, who believed she would always finish second, and continued to draw into her life other people who would only succeed at the level at which she was. The vibrations we send out attract others like us.

Does this say something about harboring prejudices against other people? Absolutely. What about talking behind people's backs and engaging in gossip which, in fact, tears other people down? These are also negativities that will only reflect back upon those that send them out. Let's say you are driving along and somebody cuts you off. Do you wave a finger of recognition at them or yell an obscenity out your car window? The problem with that is that the subconscious mind believes that you are the poor driver, rather than the other guy, and that will then weaken your own driving ability.

Our subconscious minds remember what comes out of our mouths. Even if we say something about another person, our subconscious feeds it back into our brains as if the information were about us. When we criticize another person, our subconscious mind doesn't realize we're talking about someone else; it thinks we're talking about ourselves, and we feel bad because of the negative words.

Conversely, when we say nice things about other people, such as, "You look nice," "You did a great job," or "You're really good at that," our subconscious minds hear the compliments as if they were directed at us. It's as if those compliments are for our own betterment.

There's a corollary to this: It's likely that the more you compliment other people, the less inclined you will be to issue all those negative, critical remarks.

Giving five compliments to others every day becomes a gift that is multiplied and returned to us. What we give out truly will come back tenfold. The Bible tells us that the bread that we cast upon the waters will come back to us. For purely selfish reasons, begin showing kindness to yourself by giving out five compliments a day. You'll bring a lot of happiness into the lives of others, and even more joy into your own life.

Incidentally, it's interesting to begin to pay attention to how people react when you compliment them. Compliment somebody on their hair and they discount it. Tell them you like their dress, and they'll say, "Oh, this old thing?" Mention that someone did a good job at a presentation and he'll tell you, "I'm surprised you couldn't hear my knees knocking the whole time." Most of us are so unaccustomed to hearing a compliment that we don't know how to respond.

For purely selfish reasons, begin showing kindness to yourself by giving out five compliments a day. ... Giving a compliment has the power to transform the words into reality.

Giving a compliment has the power to transform the words into reality.

My wife loves to tell the story about how we used compliments to make what could have been a miserable night out at a restaurant into a really special evening. We were out with two other couples and prepared to spend serious money on a great meal. Our plans were almost foiled, however, when we were greeted by the waitress from hell. Her first words to us were, "What do you want?" With four words she made it immediately apparent that she had a terrible attitude. Our group wanted to leave when she went to get our drinks, but we didn't move fast enough. Not only was she mean, she was quick! Before we could make a break for it, she was back slamming our glasses on the table.

I decided to use compliments to see if I could turn a surly waitress into the kind person I knew she was at heart. I told her that we were speaking about her while she went to get the drinks. The couples we were out with started to slither under the table. They were sure I was going to start a fight. I told the waitress that it was apparent that she was the best waitress in the restaurant and that we were happy to know we were going to get the best service.

After I praised her as the finest professional I could imagine and said we were so delighted she was there to help us enjoy our evening, this waitress looked at me and said, "Would you just excuse me, sir, please?" She went over to the waitress stand at the bar and said to her coworkers, "Did you hear that? They think I am the best waitress in the country. I mean, did you hear that?!?" Then she came back to us. She took our orders and went to the kitchen.

Make visible what, without you, might never have been seen.
–Robert Bresson

While she was gone, one of my friends called me a liar and asked how I could keep a straight face when I told her I felt she was the best waitress in the place. I told him that I wasn't lying—*that excellent service was within that waitress*, and I saw it as my responsibility to help her see it. That evening, we indeed had the finest service you could imagine, and when the bill came the waitress told us that we had been such a nice group that she wanted to buy us dessert.

One man told me that he complimented a grocery store clerk, then saw her helping someone else in a very positive manner. The effect of our good words can become multiplied as other people pass on the positive messages. The impact of five compliments could actually be dozens, perhaps hundreds, of kind remarks spread to people throughout the day. This was the theme of the movie "Pay It Forward," which, thankfully, was a considerable hit.

Aim for five compliments a day. If you lose count of the number of compliments you've given, start over. It's impossible to overstate how important this process will become in your life. You'll change the way you look at life, you'll change your own life, and it is very possible that you will change the life of somebody to whom you give a compliment.

You have nothing to lose and everything to gain by practicing kindness.

You Make a Difference

I heard a story recently that illustrates the importance of telling people how we feel about them. A friend e-mailed the story to me. I wish I knew the name of the author so I could share it with you. It is a beautiful story.

A teacher decided to honor each of her seniors in high school by telling them the difference they each made. She called each student to the front of the class, one at a time. First she told each of them how they had made a difference to her and the class. Then she presented each of them with a blue ribbon imprinted with gold letters that read, "Who I Am Makes a Difference." Afterwards the teacher decided to do a class project to see what kind of impact positive recognition would have on their community.

She gave each of the students three more ribbons and instructed them to go out and spread this acknowledgment ceremony. They were to follow up with specific instances of their kindness by reporting their results back to the class in about a week. One of the boys in the class went to a junior executive at a nearby company and honored him for helping the student with his career planning. The student gave the executive a blue ribbon and put it on his shirt. Then he gave the executive two extra ribbons and said, "We're doing a class project on recognition, and we'd like you to go out, find somebody to honor, and give him or her a blue ribbon. Then give that person the extra blue ribbon so he or she can acknowledge a third person and thus keep the acknowledgment ceremony going. Please contact me and tell me what happened."

Later that day the junior executive went in to see his boss, who had a reputation as being a kind of grouchy fellow. He sat the boss down and told him that he deeply admired him for being a creative genius. The boss seemed very surprised. The junior executive asked him if he would accept the gift of the blue ribbon and give him permission to put it on his lapel. His surprised boss said, "Well, sure." The junior executive took the blue ribbon and placed it right on his boss's jacket above his heart. As he gave him the last extra ribbon, he said, "Would you do me a favor? Would you take this extra ribbon and pass it on by honoring somebody else? The young boy who first gave me the ribbons is doing a project in school, and we want to keep this recognition going and find out how it affects people."

That night the boss went home to his fourteen-year-old son and sat down with him. He said, "The most incredible thing happened to me today. I was in my office, and one of the junior executives came in and told me he admired me and gave me a blue ribbon for being a creative genius. Imagine. He thinks I'm a creative genius. Then he put this blue ribbon that says 'Who I Am Makes A Difference' on my jacket above my heart. He gave me an extra ribbon and asked me to find somebody else to honor.

"As I was driving home tonight, I started thinking about whom I would honor with this ribbon, and I thought about you. I want to honor you. My days are really hectic, and when I come home I don't pay a lot of attention to you. Sometimes I

Do not save your loving speeches for your friends til they are dead; do not write them on their tombstones, speak them rather now instead.
–Anna Cummins

scream at you for not getting good enough grades in school or for your bedroom being a mess, but somehow tonight, I just wanted to sit here and, well, just let you know that you do make a difference to me. Besides your mother, you are the most important person in my life. You're a great kid, and I love you!"

The startled boy started to sob and couldn't stop crying. His whole body shook. He looked up at his father and said through his tears, "I was planning on committing suicide tomorrow, Dad, because I didn't think you loved me. Now I know you care. This is the happiest day of my life."

The boss went back to work a changed man. He was no longer a grouch, but instead made sure to let all his employees know that they made a difference. The junior executive helped several other young people with career planning and never forgot to let them know that they made a difference in his life... one of them was the boss's son. And the young boy and his classmates learned a valuable lesson. Who you are DOES make a difference.

We may never know the effect our words have on another person. You usually don't have any way of knowing what's going on in another person's life. A friend told me about the day her father died of cancer. She and her mother left the hospital after watching the person they each loved most in the world take his last breath. My friend was driving her mother home in her parents' big car. On the way home, her mother suggested they stop at the bank so they could get money to take to the funeral home to make arrangements for the burial. My friend sat in the car at the curb while her mother went inside to get some cash.

As she sat in her parents' comfortable luxury car, an angry man knocked on her window. Surprised, she rolled down the window to see what he wanted. She was shocked when he began cursing at her for parking along the curb right in front of the bank. He yelled that she was selfish and rude like all rich people, and actually spit on the car. My friend had been up all night at her father's deathbed. She was tired, and in so much pain that she was unable to even react to the man. She rolled up the window while he continued to rant at her. She hadn't thought it possible that the day of her father's death could get any worse, but this stranger made my friend feel even sadder and more hopeless than before. He was venting some inner insecurity and rage about what he perceived to be rich people who make their own rules—and in the process added to the misery of a person who was already in excruciating pain.

A thoughtless word may make a good day bad, or a terrible day more than another person can bear. A rude gesture on the highway can hurt another person's feelings, if she's already feeling bad. Smiling and letting a car into traffic ahead of you might be the only kindness another person experiences all day. It gives me a feeling of power to know that small things we do without thinking can bring happiness into another person's life.

The night Abraham Lincoln was shot, he had in his pockets five crumpled-up old pieces of paper. On each of them was written something positive that a person had said about him. Apparently, on days when Lincoln would get down in the dumps, he would reach into his pocket and pull out these pieces of paper and read them. Lincoln had been in many business relationships where his business partners had taken advantage of him. He spent much of his life paying back monies to people that had been shortchanged by his partners. And right up to his death he was relying on the power of other people's words to lift him up.

It gives me a feeling of power to know that small things we do without thinking can bring happiness into another person's life.

That is why the advice, "Lighten up, show yourself some kindness and compassion" is so important. We're harder on ourselves than anybody else would ever dream of being. But the fact is, we can turn that all around by loving ourselves from the inside out. And if we don't decide to love ourselves, why should we expect anyone else to?

Lighten up on yourself and on others. Keep the compliments flowing, and know that you are making a positive difference in other people's lives—and in your own.

Finally, here's a story about the intrinsic value that lies within each of us. A well-known speaker started his seminar by holding up a $20 bill. To the room full of 200 people, he asked, "Who would like this $20 bill?"

Hands started going up.

He said, "I am going to give this $20 bill to one of you, but first let me do this." He proceeded to crumple up the $20 bill. Then he asked, "Who still wants it?"

Still the hands went up in the air.

"Well," he replied, "what if I do this?" And he dropped it on the ground and started to grind it into the floor with his shoe. He picked it up, now crumpled and dirty. "Now, who still wants it?"

Still the hands went into the air.

"My friends, we have all learned a very valuable lesson," he said. "No matter what I did to the money, you still wanted it, because it did not decrease in value. It was still worth $20. Many times in our lives, we are dropped, crumpled, and ground into the dirt by the decisions we make and the circumstances that come our way. We feel as though we are worthless. But no matter what has happened or what will happen, you will never lose your value. Dirty or clean, crumpled or finely creased, you are priceless to those who DO LOVE you. The worth of our lives comes not in what we do or who we know, but by WHO WE ARE. You are special—don't EVER forget it."

Do all the good you can by all the means you can.
–John Wesley

Finding Your Inner Power

Continue your positive self-talk. Begin the habit of giving

five or more compliments every day to other people. Notice how many more compliments you receive once you become more generous about giving them away.

We were doing a training class and we were talking about an excellent book that I highly recommend you read, *What to Say When You Talk to Yourself,* by Shad Helmstetter (1990). There was one young lady sitting at the end of the front row with her arms tightly crossed in front of her and her legs crossed at the ankle, pulled up underneath the chair. For four solid nights she sat there in that chair, facing straight ahead. She wouldn't look at me; she wouldn't participate. It was obvious she didn't want to be there.

On the fifth night we talked a little bit, and I asked her, "Why did you come to this class?" And she said, "Because I was told I had to." And I said, "That's such a shame. I wish you would have come for other reasons." "Well," she said, "something happened last week that made me really start to get something out of this, and tonight I want to participate." That was the last class of the session.

Three months later I received a very nice letter from her thanking me for introducing her to *What to Say When You Talk to Yourself.* She said, "I read that book. It made such sense to me. I had it sent to my son. He read it, and when he was done reading it he wrote back to me and he said, 'Mom, I wish I had read this book fifteen years ago. I read it and I gave it to my cell mate. He read it, and then we passed it to the next cell and down the hall.'"

Show yourself some compassion for what you have done in the past. Appreciate that you may have done the best you could with the information you had at the time.

Notes:

List ways you could consider loving yourself more:

1.
2.
3.
4.
5.
6.
7.
8.
9.
10.

C H A P T E R   F I V E

Learning New Ways

There are many ways of going forward, but there is only one way of standing still.

—Franklin D. Roosevelt

FOR MANY PEOPLE, GOING TO SCHOOL was not a fun or rewarding experience. Many of us had teachers who condemned us, berated us or belittled us. Some of us had parents, or maybe brothers and sisters, who constantly gave us the message that we weren't very smart.

So many women tell me today that when they were girls, they were told in school they were not good at math and they never would be, because girls couldn't do math as well as boys. I can personally attest to the fact that this isn't true: one of the female divorce lawyers representing my ex-wife was a financial genius. Also, in banks and credit unions today, a high percentage of the loan officers, presidents and CEOs are women, so I know women can learn math. Most of us probably know lots of women who got beyond the negative messages they received in school to become great at math. How did they do it? And how can we get beyond the negative messages that shape our abilities to become the people we were meant to be?

One of the fastest ways to find new ways is to create a learning process in our lives. We have to start a daily diet of learning.

I have found that an important part of stepping up to claim our highest potential is finding some new ways of doing things. One of the fastest ways to find new ways is to create a learning process in our lives. We have to start a daily diet of learning. If we choose to avoid the learning process, we don't just stand still in our personal development—we actually risk falling backwards. There are so many new ways we can explore every day. Everyone with cable TV can learn from channels like the Discovery Channel, the History Channel and the Learning Channel. It may be somewhat passive learning, just watching TV, but the opportunity to learn is there.

Even the smallest communities offer training programs in many different subject areas. Whether you want to learn about computers, bridge or yoga, you can probably find a class nearby. Maybe you want to earn a college degree or perhaps your high school equivalency certificate. Find a community college or YMCA that offers the classes you want to take and sign up today. Visit your public library to check out audio and videocassette training programs. If you have a computer or can get access to one, you can find a nearly limitless supply of books, tapes and other courses to teach you just about anything you want to know. The Internet offers literally millions of opportunities to learn and grow.

We must continue to grow; without growth, we die. It is a very slow, painful death when we stop growing. Find whatever method works best for you and get started. Because I travel so much, I have lots of success with books on tape. Sometimes I use my travel time to listen to subliminal message programs to boost my confidence or help me learn something new. However, I should mention that if you plan to use subliminal tapes while you drive, make sure they're not self-hypnosis tapes. When you use an audiocassette tape or CD, you can drive along and have a personal mentor right beside you. If you get distracted in your own thoughts or have to stop listening to pay attention to something happening on the highway, hit the rewind button and your personal mentor readily teaches it to you again.

I invite you to e-mail me if you would like to acquire some of these programs at **gary@garylalonde.com**. I have quite a variety and will be happy to share with you the list of what's available.

Subliminal programs are a great way to stimulate our subconscious into helping us begin to really work toward our goals. Subliminal programs influence us by sending messages that our conscious awareness doesn't pick up. Most subliminal programs have ocean or similar soothing sounds recorded over the supportive messages designed to increase your confidence, help you stop smoking, or get rid of another bad habit or limiting belief. In subject matter, these subliminal programs go all the way from stop smoking to stop procrastinating to improving your love relationship. Your conscious mind doesn't hear the words, but subconsciously the message gets through. You can listen to subliminal messages for a prolonged period of time without increasing your stress level.

When you listen to subliminal messages, your conscious brain, or your filter, isn't engaged. Your beliefs and values can't negate the messages you're hearing. Subliminal programs let you bypass the conscious mind. Remember, our subconscious mind does not judge. When we play a subliminal program, our subconscious mind absorbs the message and accepts it as fact. This technology fell out of popular favor for a while, but is now back with a vengeance. If you want to learn more about this topic, I suggest you read *Subliminal Learning* by Eldon Taylor, Ph.D. (1998).

Whatever method you choose to learn something new, include at least some reading as part of your program. Reading uses a different part of the brain than listening does. Reading is one of the most important skills we have. Fewer than 10 percent of Americans have a library card; fewer than one percent use that card every year. Reading really gives you time to nurture yourself—to show yourself the love and respect you deserve. Reading is an integral part of our learning processes.

Another way to help you on your journey toward finding your inner power is to let other people help you. Maybe your spouse, partner, a parent, a child or a friend can help you find some new ways. Benjamin Franklin once remarked that the quickest way to cement a friendship is to let another person do a favor for you.

Here's an example of how some acquaintances helped me find a new way. I used to be a white-knuckle flyer. I was terrified of flying in airplanes. During my drinking days I would spend $30 or $40 in the airport bar just to give me enough liquid courage to get on the plane. Once on the plane, I badgered the flight attendants to keep the liquor coming. I'm sure I made them, and most of the people seated near me, pretty miserable during those flights.

Once I had taken my first steps toward changing my life, I decided to find a new way to fly. At a Tony Robbins seminar I was attending, I heard that some people at the seminar were going skydiving. At that point I thought skydiving was for poor souls who didn't know enough not to jump out of a perfectly secure airplane. I thought nobody in his right mind would do this. But I was at the point in my personal development at which I was searching for some new ways.

Pushing down all the fear in my heart, I asked the group if there was room for me on the skydiving trip. I got the courage to ask to go because I had heard that the trip was full. I felt sure they would say no, and I got my wish—they told me they were sorry, but the trips were fully booked. They promised to call if there were any cancellations.

Boy, I was so happy they were full.

I had shown some courage and strength by talking about how I wanted to go and do the parachute jump, so that helped an ego need that I had. On the other hand, my inner fears that were resisting doing the jump were also satisfied because there was no place for me in line.

As it so happened, that afternoon Tony Robbins chose me to join him on the stage at the seminar and helped me deal with another phobia, the fear of water. I had almost drowned as a child. After I overcame my fear of water that day, I knew I could break through my fear of flying. It was a good thing, because that afternoon I found out there was room for me on the skydiving trip. It was the most exhilarating experience I have ever had. The next day I phoned home to ask my wife to wire $250 so I could go skydiving again.

No bird soars too high if he soars with his own wings.
–William Blake

"Again?!" she asked. "What do you mean, again?" She couldn't believe I had done it, so on the second trip I hired a skydiver to videotape me as I plummeted to earth safely. I showed her the tape to prove that I had done it, and now I replay the tape whenever I need to confront another fear in my life. It helps to reinforce what I have learned.

Doing What We Fear

All of us have fears to overcome. I'm not talking about logical, reasonable fears that protect us from danger. There's a reason that we don't leap from tall buildings or leave our doors unlocked at night. I'm talking about the day-to-day experiences from which we hide—fears like talking to strangers or speaking in front of a group. Sometimes the stranger you fear may be your next best friend just waiting to meet you. Don't deprive yourself by shutting out such opportunities.

Bill Gates, Thomas Edison and the Wright brothers put

themselves on the line, and what they accomplished has made life better for all of us. That's what finding some new ways can do for us. It can give us the courage to do what we need to do. We just have to realize that we have it inside us to do what we need to do.

The ultimate way to realize you *can* do it is *to* DO IT.

You must persevere long enough to get past the initial objections your "limited thinking" mind might provide: the objection that "your old ways were better," that the "uncomfortable feeling of change isn't very nice," and all the other lies we allow ourselves to buy into. Once you step past those lies, the actual act of doing it can become fun. I know this because I was raised to believe that children should be seen, not heard. When I first began speaking to large groups of people, it was terrifying. I used to ask the dry cleaner to starch the legs of my suit so my knees couldn't be seen shaking.

Learning helps us to build the courage to take the fifth step in our personal breakthrough—the step of finding some new ways to do things. Learning lays the foundation. It is still up to you to take the next step. You have to do it; no one else can do it for you. You have to be willing to do what it takes. Initially, the new ways you choose will not be as comfortable to you as the old ways that made up your "comfort zone." If you take several small steps, eventually you may find yourself in a place where you can look back and SEE just how uncomfortable that zone was.

We have to step beyond our comfort zones if we want to grow.

Incidentally, I think it's ironic that most of our "comfort" zones are so painful. Being part of a couple becomes a comfort zone for some people. We become afraid to leave that comfort zone, even after the relationship goes bad. The problem is that very little growth ever occurs within a comfort zone. We have to step beyond our comfort zones if we want to grow. Finding the power that lives inside you involves breaking out of your painful comfort zone to achieve your highest potential.

When you think about it, the term "comfort zone" is such a misnomer. Have you ever hit that little bone at the bottom of your elbow? They call it "the funny bone," but does it make you laugh when you hit it? Far from it. It's painful as can be. And that's the same thing with our so-called "comfort zone." We've been led to believe that we're "comfortable" in there, but actually we're not. It really ought to be called our "discomfort zone."

Having been in sales for many years and having worked with thousands of salespeople around the world, I can confidently state a truth about sales: at one time or another, all salespeople become terrified of the telephone. No matter how successful they are or have been, most salespeople develop a fear of what will happen when they make a phone call. They're certain they'll be rejected, yelled at or hung up on. Every salesperson will tell you that these things do happen to them. Sometimes they happen every day. But they'll also tell you that sometimes the person on the other end of the phone will place an order, inquire about a new product or make a referral to another potential customer. The only way to get to the person who wants to place an order with us is to make the call. Maybe you'll be rejected, but to get the order, successful salespeople know they have to get past the things they're afraid of doing.

It is only by risking from one hour to another that we live at all.
–William James

Eleanor Roosevelt put it like this: *"We can experience a true sense of freedom by doing the thing we fear doing the most. I gain strength and courage by every experience in which I must stop and look fear in the face... I say to myself, I've lived through this and can take the next thing that comes along... We must do the things we cannot do."*

To help salespeople face their fear and do the things they think they cannot do, I suggest that they set a daily goal. It may mean calling five people, or ten or twenty, but making the commitment to make the calls every day is the key. At first, doing this might be torturous. You may get through to only one or two people the first day. But getting through to these people will give you the confidence to try again; eventually you'll make twenty calls and end up talking with ten customers or prospects.

Make Your Goals a Reality

By now you understand that there is a process to change. You know it's important to live in the here and now. You know how important it is to give yourself the RIGHT messages when you talk to yourself. You know that negative self-talk keeps the wisdom of the universe from flowing through you. Most of us have spent much more energy and time talking ourselves out of the blessings we want, than talking ourselves into what we deserve. Words are powerful, so when you recognize that you may have been standing in your own way, don't beat yourself up about it.

Recognize that what you had been doing wasn't working. Find some new ways to do it and then move forward. Be gentle with yourself. As Vernon Howard stated, "When you find yourself in the storm of life, remember -- you're the storm." Don't tell yourself that you've been stupid all these years because you couldn't find the way to get ahead at work. Acknowledge that you have learned what doesn't work and congratulate yourself for recognizing this. See the glass as half full rather than half empty.

Life was meant to be lived and curiosity must be kept alive. One must never, for whatever reason, turn his back on life.
–Eleanor Roosevelt

We all need to find new ways to make our personal development goals, our New Year's resolutions, our sales objectives happen. If you understand this, you'll become part of the elite who understand what they want and know how to make it reality.

You can change your life. You can take control and bring about the positive changes you desire. Most of us spend so much of our lives on automatic pilot. The fifth step asks you to release yourself from automatic pilot. Get rid of the habits you've rehearsed your whole life and find some new ways. Keep learning. There is so much power in knowledge. You're only using a tiny portion of your knowledge and brain. Find a subject you want to learn more about and start learning. It may not be easy, but it will get you started. It's a new way. If you want to succeed, you'll have to find some new ways.

Give these suggestions a try. Get out of bed every day with some power and excitement in your life. Give compliments every time you can. People who sit in tollbooths or gas station kiosks are usually bored to death and dying for conversation. Thank one of them for coming to work today. Seek out the owner of a restaurant and thank him for hiring such great people. Go the extra mile for people. You'll be surprised at the rewards you reap when you start going out of your way to help other people. Then you'll realize that you have learned a new way of taking care of yourself.

> *You'll be surprised at the rewards you reap when you start going out of your way to help other people.*

Now you can see how the learning process is a key step in your breakthrough. The first steps are huge, but until we begin finding new ways, new steps, new thoughts, we'll stay frozen in our comfort zone—in our pain.

Finding Your Inner Power

Read *From a Chicken to an Eagle,* by Jerry Frankhauser (1983). If your local bookstore can't order this book, visit our website at www.garylalonde.com and click on "Request Catalogue." It's a short book, but the message is life changing! It will take you on an important journey. Most of us live our lives as chickens when we were destined to be eagles. This book will help you find some new ways to tap your inner power.

Find new ways to meet your needs. Change will often expose an unmet need. Take your needs *seriously* and you'll discover new ways to meet them. This will harness change for your benefit.

Notes:

Break out of automatic pilot and find new avenues for learning (books, tapes, seminars). Make a list below of resources you have identified and plan to explore:

1.
2.
3.
4.
5.
6.
7.
8.
9.
10.

C H A P T E R S I X

Building Support Groups

A dwarf standing on the shoulders of a giant may see farther than a giant himself.
—Robert Burton

DO YOU HAVE A SUPPORT SYSTEM? Do you have a support partner, someone you can call when you're in trouble—even more importantly, someone you can call when you're really full of joy? Are you part of someone else's support system? Are you a strong support partner? I am blessed to have a great support system. The most important part of my support system is my wife. I am very blessed to have met my soul mate in her. She provides support for me through the good times and the bad. Why is support so important?

Picture yourself looking at a fire. Imagine twelve logs in the fire burning cheerfully. If you take a pair of iron tongs and remove one of the logs, what will happen to the fire? The remaining eleven logs will go on burning, but the one you removed will soon burn out. Some of us are living like the lone log. We work in a little cubicle or office, we come home and many of us eat alone, then plop down in front of the TV or go online for much of the evening. Where are the relationships? Where is the support system?

If you want to make changes in your life, it's very important to develop a strong support system. You need somebody to be there for you, and you need to be there for others. Remember how rewarding it can be to help someone else. Being part of a strong support system can change your whole life. In his excellent book *Dig Your Own Well Before You're Thirsty* (1997), Harvey McKay recommends being proactive about preparing for tough times. We need to brace ourselves by building a strong support system.

One of the first things I suggest you do when you begin to look for some support is to become keenly aware of the environment that surrounds you. Think of the people you interact with at home, at work, or when you're relaxing. Are they positive people who make you feel good about life? Do you feel uplifted by them? Or are they oozing negative energy? Are they always complaining about something?

Most of us know people who can't wait to share bad news. They love to gossip, especially when the gossip involves others' misfortune. These are the people who can't wait to tell you who's getting a divorce, who's having money problems, who just got fired. Sometimes these people exaggerate or outright lie about other people. I think it's the only way these negative people can see to make themselves feel better about their own lives. A negative person is like the man with the muck rake in *Pilgrims' Progress*. He is so intent on grubbing around in the mud at his feet that he never looks up to see the beauty of the stars overhead.

There's a story about a world traveler who happens upon a small valley whose beauty just mesmerizes him. One of the old locals comes out to greet him, and when the traveler remarks about how beautiful the place is, the local says, "True, but you should see it in springtime with the rains and the melting snow. Every year we have torrential floods that just wipe out our whole village. We have to rebuild it all." The wise traveler asks, "Do you love the village?" The resident says, "Yes." And then the traveler suggests, "Then why don't you build your houses up just a little higher on the ridge? You'd all have a better view, and you would sit high and dry above the flooding."

The lesson is: Stop being so negative; the solution is right in front of your nose if you'll look up to see it.

Negative people suck the life out of everyone with whom they come in contact. After spending time with a person like this, you may feel deflated, like a balloon that has lost all of its air. If you're trying to find your inner power, the people with whom you associate can be of great help to you. On the other hand, they can also be a great hindrance in your achieving what you desire. Choose your companions carefully. Finding some positive friends will give you a terrific start on a healthy support system.

If you're trying to find your inner power, the people with whom you associate can be of great help to you. ... Finding some positive friends will give you a terrific start on a healthy support system.

Words of Encouragement

All of us need to hear words of encouragement. Whom do you turn to when you need some positive strokes? Many of us are lucky enough to have loving, supportive people in our families. But it's sad that, in too many cases, we can't turn to family for support. Who will give you the words of encouragement that will propel you closer to your goal? Keep in mind the value and significance of a support system, and consider the people in your life. Do they exude positive or negative energy? This is the energy that will spill over into you.

As I make presentations throughout the country, I am blessed to meet so many positive, energizing people. My friend Linda is one of these folks. She shimmers with positive energy. Linda always wants only the best for other people. Even on her down days, when she is facing business or personal challenges,

Linda's energy is so HIGH that she has a positive impact on everyone she meets. Linda has built an advertising agency that has become one of the most successful in her state. Part of the reason is her positive nature, and not just with her clients and potential clients. Linda makes everyone around her feel like an important part of the team.

Every time someone in her office signs a new client, wins an award or has an event like a birthday or anniversary, Linda gathers her whole staff together by beating on a child's tom-tom. Once the group gathers, she shares the good news and leads a round of cheers. Does that sound like grade school? The people who work with Linda don't feel as if they're in grade school. They feel extremely lucky to work in such a warm and caring atmosphere. They feel cherished and appreciated, and Linda's company has very little staff turnover. A nice bonus is that the company is very successful. I'm convinced it's because of the cheerful, positive environment Linda has created. It nurtures the creativity of the staff, and frees them to achieve great things personally and professionally.

Do you surround yourself with people like Linda? I believe that you can tell a lot about a person by looking at the people around him or her. Most of us seek out people like ourselves. Take a quick look at the people in your life. It will give you a mirror into your own beliefs and value system.

When we begin to step towards our higher, better selves, having a negative support system is not in our best interest. It may be time to find some new, positive support. I'm not suggesting for a second that you sever relationships with people who have been in your life for a long time. But if you're truly serious about breaking through to your highest potential, you may want to spend less time with some of those negative people. That way you'll be less likely to absorb some of their ailments.

Do an inventory of the people in your life, and pay attention to the time you spend with people who drain others' energy. We want to create relationships with those who have visions and goals, a strong purpose and passion in their life. Find out what it is that allows them to fuel that passion and continue to move forward. Most people who have high energy and passion are looking to support others to achieve their own highest good. My friend Linda makes a living at looking for the best in others.

Genius is mainly an affair of energy.
–Matthew Arnold

Cable magnate Bill Turner's cancer was so advanced when it was discovered that it probably would have killed most people. But Bill remained at the helm of Turner Vision practically until his death, with the goal of empowering humankind. I believe his positive outlook was one of his strongest weapons against his illness.

Bill Turner eventually did succumb to the disease, but he lived much longer than he'd been expected to. And he kept his environment positive throughout. He surrounded himself with people who had beat cancer themselves and others who could bring him the best remedies from alternative medicine. It was just phenomenal what his support group was able to do for him.

We Empower Ourselves When We Empower Others

Have you ever noticed what happens when you touch a burning candle to the wick of an unlit candle? The flame burns brighter. Then, when you take away the second candle, they each continue to burn brightly. The first candle hasn't lost anything by giving flame to the second candle.

I have been privileged to provide a great deal of training for the wonderful people who work with Mary Kay, a company that truly exemplifies this idea of passing on the flame to others. Under the guidance of its founder, Mary Kay Ash, this company has done so much to help women in this country and around the world. Selling cosmetics is just a small part of their mission.

Consider Mary Kay's mission statement:

Mary Kay's mission is to enrich women's lives. We will do this in tangible ways, by offering quality products to consumers, financial opportunities to our independent sales force and fulfilling careers to our employees.

We also will reach out to the heart and spirit of women, enabling personal growth and fulfillment for the women whose lives we touch.

We will carry out our mission in a spirit of caring, living the positive values on which our Company was built.

This sounds more like a personal philosophy than a corporate mission statement. But Mary Kay Ash created a multinational corporation with this philosophy. Today Mary Kay is the best-selling brand of skin care and color cosmetics in the United States. In addition to empowering the more than 650,000 independent representatives (most of whom are women), Ms. Ash founded a non-profit, public foundation to fund research to fight cancers affecting women.

This philosophy provides an energy that allows Mary Kay consultants to put in long days and approach many more people. Selling is hard work—especially for someone who may have been out of the job market for a long time. Many consultants are women who have never worked outside the home and don't have confidence that they can become successful. But Mary Kay provides training and support to help sales consultants feel good about themselves, their appearance and their experience. Her company helps them tap into their inner wisdom to help other women.

We may affirm absolutely that nothing great in the world has been accomplished without passion.
–Hegel

The Mary Kay consultants I have been privileged to work with are women with a purpose and a passion in their lives. They are some of the most positive people I have ever met. Through their "go-give" approach, they enjoy helping other women while they make a living for themselves and their families.

Mary Kay consultants stay in close touch with one another to give and receive ideas and support. If you don't have a network of support like this, it's time to build one for yourself. You can change your life by finding friends and co-workers who are positive.

Dealing with Negativity

But what happens when the person closest to you is anything but positive? Many of the people I have worked with experience a real crisis when they realize that the biggest downer in their network of negative feedback is their significant other. I don't want to understate the difficulty you can face if your spouse or life partner is constantly negative.

If the most important person in your life is always negative, he or she is almost certainly holding you back. Getting a constant stream of negativity from the most important person in one's life would hold anybody back. What's so interesting about this is that this negativity is usually a demonstration of the spouse's own fears and insecurities. The negativity can be your spouse's way of exercising control over your behavior.

If the most important person in your life is always negative, he or she is almost certainly holding you back.

For example, one woman with whom I worked wanted to go on a weight reduction program. She started preparing healthier foods for the family and began an energetic walking program. She thought her husband would be pleased that she was trying to improve her health and her appearance, but soon found the opposite was true. He actively discouraged her from pursuing her weight reduction goals. From the very beginning, he was giving her negative messages. "You'll never walk that weight off," he would say. "Why are you trying this again? You'll just fail." He even went so far as to bring home her favorite high-calorie foods to tempt her off her diet.

I think negative people like this man are really screaming, "I wish I could do what you want to do, but if I let you be successful at what you want to do, you may just leave me because you'll no longer need me." He was literally afraid that she was going to outgrow him and be stronger or more capable than he. In this particular case, he was so insecure that he feared if she got her figure back, she'd find somebody who would treat her better than he would. It could be the same when one partner tries to go back to school, get a better job or make any kind of positive change in his or her life.

I'm sorry to tell you that there's no magical solution for people with negative spouses or partners. In some cases the spouse's fear is so deep that nothing will move him or her away from that fear. The good news is that people who want to change their lives in a positive way can do it and still respect their partners. They can do this by making the changes in their lives they want to make and by showing understanding and compassion to the spouse who may resent the changes. Tell your spouse, "I'll respect you. Please respect me. I won't try to change you. Please don't try to change me."

A very negative spouse may say harsh and unkind things to you in a vain attempt to bring you back into his or her comfort zone. Just tell your partner that the negative approach is not acceptable to you anymore, and ask him or her to use only a positive approach. Explain that at one point in your life the negative approach was acceptable—now it isn't. By stating how you want your mate to speak to you, you're showing him or her how to be more positive and providing him or her with the support he or she is really looking for.

You can usually rise above a negative relationship, as long as it's only verbally negative. If you find yourself in a physically abusive relationship, however, you need to get help. Physical abuse will break down your self-esteem to the point that you can actually believe you deserve such treatment.

We all have fears and insecurities. I believe it is our mission to grow through experiencing these challenges. To do this, in some cases, you may need to find support outside of your home. A neighbor, colleague or friend might be interested in joining you in pursuing a similar goal. If your goal is weight reduction, for example, and you don't know anybody personally who would desire the same goal, try Weight Watchers or a similar support program. When you find the courage and strength to continue and you begin to reach your goals, you may find that your negative spouse will change his or her mind and join you in your program.

Here's a critical point for those of you who do want to change your weight. So many times we tell ourselves and others that, "I'm going to go on a diet and I'm going to LOSE weight." The important thing to know and to remember is that our brain has been conditioned from an early age that whatever we lose, we need to go and find—or replace, be it a textbook or a school paper or our keys. Whatever it was, we were always told to go and find it. So every time we diet and succeed, we tell friends and ourselves that we've "lost weight." The subconscious mind is conditioned in such a way that when it hears "lost," it says, "Go find it!" Therefore, the body goes out seeking the weight that has been lost, and many times it not only finds what was lost, but it also finds extra. Remember that when you do a weight reduction program, avoid using the word "lost" to describe your success. Just say you *reduced* your weight, or you achieved *a better weight.*

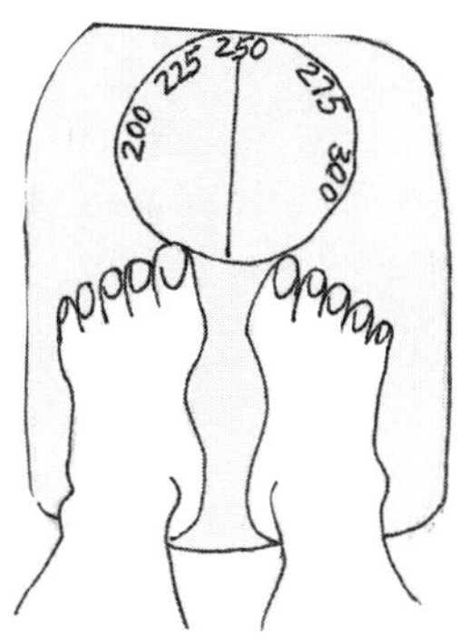

Support Groups are Powerful

Sometimes it's impossible to get support from the people you're spending time with. I used to belong to a large group of heavy drinkers. One of our friends decided to quit drinking, and we couldn't believe it. Michael decided to go on the wagon after his wife threatened to divorce him and take everything he had unless he stopped. This man truly had a lot to lose by being divorced, and he knew in his heart that his drinking was out of control. He decided, then and there, to stop drinking. We teased him and made fun of him and encouraged him to ignore his wife, but he stayed strong. Without any support from us, he achieved a year of sobriety. About that time, another member of this group decided to do the same thing. I was scared that I was losing my best drinking buddy.

Thirty days after Denny quit drinking, I made the decision to join him. I have been a non-drinker for more than fifteen years, and I owe it all to Michael and Denny, my friends who had the desire and courage to make the change. Something happened when I changed the type of people I associated with and the environment I circulated in. The balance of our group teased us and harassed us and eventually dropped us from their circle of friends. For me this was very painful. As I stopped drinking, I was very fearful of losing that sphere of influence. However, that negative circle of friends has been replaced, at least one hundredfold, by people who know how to live positively and creatively. Now I'm no longer locked in the self-sabotaging lifestyle I had been living for so many years.

As I think of this story with Michael, Denny and me, I can see the progression that took place. As we moved along our life paths, we not only created within ourselves a new support system, we also became support systems for others. I was amazed at the number of people who quit drinking after I did. They later told me that when they saw that I had done it, they knew they could do it too. I was doubly blessed to have been their catalyst for change.

People who want to change their lives have many exciting choices. If you don't know somebody who can model the positive change you desire, seek help in a support group. There are so many support groups available today for people who want to bring positive changes into their lives. Dale Carnegie programs help people gain personal confidence. Alcoholics Anonymous and other twelve-step anonymous fellowship groups help people to stop drinking, gambling, overeating and many other negative behaviors. Seek and you shall find.

Many people find it comfortable to start with their church, temple, mosque or synagogue. Church programs help immerse people in environments of love that don't exist in many homes. The Unity Church near my home has a number of different empowering programs going on at any given time, for all age groups. The church does not use these programs to promote its religious beliefs; it offers the programs as a public service.

Another way of getting the support you need is to surround yourself with people you respect. You can create your own support group that consists of people with whom you make a commitment to meet once each week for an hour or so. The time and place should be the same every week so people in your group can build the meeting into their schedules. Use this time to find out what your friends are working on, and you can share with them what you're attempting to achieve. Then the members of your group provide positive support for you, as you do for them.

Here's how one mutual support group I know does it. Each week, every member of the group says something such as, "Gary, I affirm your efforts to achieve your important goal. I see you achieving your goal, and I see you helping many other people as you achieve it. Through your efforts, you're bringing so many positive things into the universe." Your support group may not be this formal. It may just consist of stopping after class with a group of friends to share some refreshments and discuss what happened in class that night. You each will get a chance to blow off steam, discuss any problems you're having in the course, talk about assignments and offer any help you can.

Two people I know support each other by starting every day with a forty-five-minute walk or run. They bundle their kids off to school, and before they start work they walk together. The exercise is good for them, and the time away from work and family gives them a chance to get things off their chest and use each other as a sounding board.

Starting your own support group can really propel you forward in your efforts to find your inner power. So how do you get started? Think about somebody you know who is actually doing something that is making a difference. Maybe he's working with underprivileged children. Or he could be changing his eating and exercise habits as he recovers from a heart attack. Call him up and tell him that you're really proud of the time and energy he is putting into achieving his goal. Tell him that you'd like to get together with him and a couple of other people each week to support each other as you work to achieve your goals.

Whether you get it from your family, from an established group, from your own support group or through religious affiliation, you'll find that your path is much easier with support.

It needs to be said that you may be able to achieve your goal without support, but the effort it will take is enormous. With the right support, all things are possible. Support is so powerful. Whether you get it from your family, from an established group, from your own support group or through religious affiliation, you'll find that your path is much easier with support. It's tough to do it alone, but YOU DON'T HAVE TO! If you look carefully enough, you will find that there are always people at hand who will help you to help yourself.

Many times, however, we won't ask people to help us because we don't think we're worthy of their love and support. The sad thing is that the people you want to ask may be the people who are on the verge of doing what you want to do.

Chances are, they want to help others help themselves. It amazes me that we won't ask for help when the people we want to ask are so willing to help us.

A number of years ago, I heard there was a man in Ann Arbor, Michigan, who was the world's largest reseller of Digital Equipment Computers, and I thought to myself, "Wow, that's phenomenal, the world's largest! I'd like to meet him." So I started calling his office and leaving with his secretary requests to meet with him. She kept saying, "Gary, what's this about?" and I said, "Mr. Newman knows something I need to know. I'm just asking for him to point me in the right direction."

I kept calling, and nothing happened. She wouldn't put me through to him or get me on his calendar. It occurred to me that quite possibly, when the secretary was on her lunch break, Mr. Newman might answer his own phone. I wondered what time this lady went to lunch. So I started calling at 11:00—she was still there; 11:15—she was still there; 11:45—still there. It turned out that she went to lunch from 12:15 to 1:15.

Only those who risk going too far can possibly find out how far one can go.
–T.S. Eliot

One day he picked up his own phone and I got through to Mr. Newman. When he heard why I wanted to meet him he said, "Gary, you've overestimated my accomplishments." He was a very humble man. But I said, "Sir, I really don't believe so. Is it possible for us to meet?" And that's how I got in to see him.

I told him I wanted to build a business of speaking and training and helping people and added, "You've taken a commodity here that anybody can have, and you've built it into the largest operation in your sector. I'm attempting to do something similar with my business." He asked, "What's your plan?" And I knew he'd want to talk more. Not only did he give me an appointment, he ended up taking me to dinner. His generosity and his talent just flowed out in his efforts to help me. Isn't that something?

Oftentimes we may feel inadequate or hesitant about asking help from someone who is obviously very accomplished. All the time, however, many such people are just waiting to be asked for help from someone on the way up.

When you ask a person for help, keep in mind that he or she may not be the right person to help you. However, because you had the courage to ask, if that person can't help you, he or she may be able to introduce you to a person who can.

Getting Environmental Support

People aren't the only influence in our lives. Our environment also contributes to our ability to make meaningful changes. Many things, like the music we listen to, the news programs we watch and the magazines we read, can have a powerful impact on us. The sound of others talking around us—the people in the office, the commuters behind us on the train—also affects us. All of these external things become part of the environment around us, for good or bad. Many of them occur and we're not even remotely aware they're affecting us.

As you go about your life today, cultivate awareness of the kinds of things you're exposed to. Are you hearing positive, supportive messages, or do you have a steady diet of crime, sorrow and negativity? If you're not getting positive messages from the people, the music or the news media to which you're exposing yourself, it's time to make some changes.

Finding Your Inner Power

Examine the support system you currently have. Write down the names of the five people you are most involved with. Next to each name write an honest assessment of their energy. Is it positive or negative? Are the people you listed satisfied with where they are going? Are they excited to be actively involved in their own and others' lives? Do these people energize you or drain you? If you find that some of the people on your list are energy drainers, make it a point TODAY to spend less time with them.

If you find that you are indeed involved with a life partner who has a negative personality, make a commitment to your own growth today to tell that person you need his or her respect in working toward the goals that are important to you. Offer your respect; let your mate know you are not interested in changing him or her, but that you only ask to be respected in return. Ask that your partner not work hard to negate your own efforts.

Then decide what avenue would work best for you in building your own support network. Would you prefer to work within a group or an individual setting? If you would prefer a group, set your goal and find a group affiliated with the goal. Begin researching groups in your area, and consider the possibility of forming one if one isn't available to suit your needs.

If you would prefer an individual contact, then find a mentor. Find someone you admire; call him or her today and tell him that you do! Ask your mentor if he'd be able to offer assistance in reaching your specific goals.

The bottom line of this exercise is to cultivate awareness of the support system you currently have, and to realize its importance in helping you reach your goal or hindering you from ever getting there. Once you've realized that, you must work on limiting it to contain people who can support you and help you move only forward, only upward!

Get yourself some support. The environment you live in and the people you see affect your ability to make a change. Respect the power of their influence. Surround yourself with supportive people and create an environment that fosters positive change.

Notes:

Start a list of people (near or far) who could be part of your support group:

1.
2.
3.
4.
5.
6.
7.
8.
9.
10.

C H A P T E R   S E V E N

Sustaining the Effort

Nothing in this world can take the place of persistence. Talent will not; nothing is more common than unsuccessful people with talent. Genius will not; unrewarded genius is almost a proverb. Education will not; the world is full of educated derelicts. Persistence and determination alone are omnipotent. The slogan "press on" has solved and always will solve the problems of the human race.

—Calvin Coolidge

HOW LONG DOES CHANGE TAKE? It's different for every person. The journey is as individual and unique as the traveler. Your path to change is different from mine, and it will differ from your partner's.

One spring a woman asked me to help her with a weight problem. I asked her to call me when she was ready. She called me in December. As we worked together, she was able to enter her subconscious mind and change some of the files that had been stored there for twenty-one years. By changing those files, she reduced her weight by 170 pounds. I received a fax recently from another lady telling me she had given 108 pounds back into the universe.

My gift to you is this: imagine I give you one tiny Chinese bamboo seed. It is up to you to plant the seed. See that your pot has the most fertile soil imaginable. Know that anything will grow, at any time of year. Once you plant your seed, you must commit to watering it every day. For two years you may water your seed but find that you see nothing except wet soil.

Your family, your friends and your neighbors may begin to think you are crazy. Simply put yourself in a place of trust and keep watering your seed. After a time, still nothing may happen. KEEP WATERING! For four years you keep watering and nothing appears above ground. Yet again, I say, KEEP WATERING! You find yourself at the beginning of the fifth year, and WHAM!!! Your Chinese bamboo jumps a mighty ninety feet toward the heavens. What happened, you ask? It took time for the plant to develop strong roots. Only after the roots were established and took hold, did the bamboo find the power to BREAK THROUGH! The power was always there; it just needed to be nurtured.

Our mind is like the bamboo seed. Although to those around us, it may appear that nothing is happening on the surface, we must build or re-build our "roots," our own strong foundation. Our foundation consists of the thoughts we think and the beliefs we hold about others and ourselves. KEEP WATERING! Keep reading, keep focused on your goals, keep using your support network, and keep your self-talk positive.

All this has tremendous application to people starting businesses. Most people start a business that is relatively small and then they talk about having "a small business." Conceivably, this could be part of the problem right there, because as long as you have in your mind that you run a small business, it may just stay small.

There are many reasons for business failure, but one that is not cited very often, and that is probably the main reason, is simply that people give up. Maybe they have a cash flow problem, which is one of the reasons people cite for businesses not working. Maybe they are undercapitalized, another common reason given for business failure. But those aren't the real reason. The real reason is that people throw in the towel. People expect the bamboo shoot to be up there in two years or less, but possibly it's going to take seven or more years, and they don't understand that.

The sad thing of it is, this is part of the conditioning we receive in our society of instant lottos and instant potatoes. It's no wonder that most people who start businesses quit. They stop because initially a business is extremely demanding. We've all heard the old analogy about a jet taking off from the airport—60 percent of the fuel on board is used just getting that plane into the air. A new business can prove very gratifying. It can also test you emotionally, physically, and spiritually, way beyond what you thought it might. If people would just allow for that challenge, and make themselves ready to take it on, we would have far fewer business failures.

And that description of yourself as "just having a small business" has got to go. I was very blessed early in life to meet somebody far more talented with computers than I could ever wish to be, and he made me a big sign that read, "Business is Booming." It now hangs over the top of the closet in my bedroom. Down the sign it spells out "Premiere Performance."

We must sail, sometimes with the wind and sometimes against it–but we must sail, and not drift, nor lie at anchor.
–Oliver Wendell Holmes, Jr.

That's how we should talk about our business to other people—"It's booming," "It's successful," "It's unbelievable"—even at those times when it's not, and then, like this Chinese bamboo tree seed, continue to water the passion, the goal, the dream. And how long it will take for you may very well be different than for me.

People who start out with a concept that the business *must* be successful within two years are self-defeating. They could very well be setting themselves to be out of business in eighteen months because they see that "it's not happening."

Mark Victor Hansen, bless his heart, was the only person that stayed with me when I was even thinking of quitting. And he said to me early on, "So, you want to be a big speaker, do you?" And I said, "Mark, it's not that I want to be, it's that I *have* to be. I have come from the dark, the despair, the despondency, and I'm coming into the light, and I need other people to know there is light." And here's what he said to me—and I did not understand the impact of it at the time: "Gary," he said, "you will have it, and you will have it greater and grander than your wildest imagination—if you just don't quit."

Never give up, for that is just the place and time that the tide will turn.
–Harriet Beecher Stowe

Although I heard the words, I didn't know there would be lawsuits, or a business manager who would run my business into the ground. I didn't know that some people close to me would die, and that other people, through their fears and jealousies, would steal from me. Attached to my computer screen today, however, is a statement that says, "Success seems to be a matter of hanging on longer than the others."

So quitting is not an option…as long as you are clear in your mind that you are doing what you should be doing. Now you may, quite reasonably, decide that you have gone off on the wrong track, and that you may need to rethink your commitment to a business or a profession. That's different.

There was a young fellow who had built a dry cleaning operation in a good location, and a friend of mine used to take his clothes there to be cleaned. One day my friend saw a sign on the cleaners: "Business for sale." And he said to the young owner-manager, "What's the matter? I see lots of people coming here; you do a good job on dry cleaning, and are you not making a lot of money or whatever? Is there something wrong with your location?"

"No," the owner said, "I just don't feel like doing this. This is not the kind of business I want to do for the rest of my life."

Now that kind of quitting I can understand. It wasn't that this man was unsuccessful; it was that he was figuring out this occupation was not the way he wanted to spend his life.

You Too Can Break Through!

I have mentioned that Mark Victor Hansen, co-author of the *Chicken Soup*® books, is one of my mentors. I felt compelled to share what I have learned with others, so I ventured into the leadership training business. When I began, Mark gave me some important advice. He told me to stick with it... no matter what. There were times, especially when I was first starting out, that I wanted to chuck it all and look for another job working for somebody else. Money was tight. I envied people at the grocery store who had food stamps because they were able to feed their families better than I.

In the end, I'm really glad that I stuck with it. If I had given up, I would never have met the Gary that I am today. A huge shift resulted. I went from being a taker and a user to being a giver. Some of the sweetest things that have ever happened to me occurred after I helped someone, with no expectation of return, but simply for the sheer joy of doing it.

Our world works within the principles of synergy. What you put out into the universe comes back to you. When you put energy out over a sustained period of time, it is sure to come back to you, multiplied. When you help one person, you're tithing to God, and your reward will come from within his creation, though not necessarily from the person for whom you did the favor.

Some of the sweetest things that have ever happened to me occurred after I helped someone, with no expectation of return, but simply for the sheer joy of doing it.

I remember a family that illustrated this point beautifully. It was graduation day. The daughter was the first person in her entire family to graduate from college. Her parents were so happy and proud. The daughter was so very grateful for the sacrifices her parents had made to send her to college. She didn't have to take any student loans or even work while she went to college, because her parents had scrimped and saved for years.

As she stood after graduation with her diploma in hand and tears in her eyes, she said to her parents, "How will I ever be able to thank you enough? How can I ever pay you back?" Her parents hugged her, and I heard her father say in a shaky voice, "You can pay us back by passing it on. We were privileged to be able to do this for you. I hope you have the privilege of doing it for your children, or for someone else."

I know that the daughter has worked hard to pass on the gifts she got from her parents. While she doesn't have any children, she and her husband have hosted a series of exchange students from other countries, providing them with a happy home while they study in the U.S. And they always tell the students, "You don't owe us anything. We just hope you can pass on this kindness to others someday." In this way, the kindness her parents showed her has been multiplied many times over and has been felt around the world.

You can achieve the same kind of impressive results if you make a goal, stick with it, and accept help from whatever source offers it. I am happy to be able to share with you a letter from a woman whom I was privileged to meet when she attended one of my learning experiences. As you will see by the letter, she faced an enormous number of what most people would consider setbacks during a very short time. She was persistent, however, and the results have been unbelievable. Here's the letter:

Dear Gary,

I am writing in gratitude for the Pacesetters class you taught at the Hilton in Akron, Ohio. I can't even begin to tell you how it has changed and deeply touched my life. I am forever changed, and I will be eternally grateful.

In May of this year, I had momentum going in my business. I was almost on target for the car and had momentum going to do great things. On May 6, I found out a dear elderly friend had passed away. Little Mary, as I called her, was like a grandma to me. I was heart-broken, but I knew she was in Heaven. On May 10, I found out the baby I was carrying (six months) was very ill. They had given us a 99% chance of a stillbirth. The details are not important, but my husband and I lost our son on May 26. Nothing in this world, in my opinion, can match the grief of losing a child. I was so devastated that I merely existed for months. Recently, my mother-in-law was diagnosed with breast cancer, a survivor-in-the-making. Also, my husband's company is shutting down on January 4. I told God I understood being tested, but I thought this was getting out of hand.

Strength does not come from winning. Your struggles develop your strengths. When you go through hardships and decide not to surrender, that is strength.
–Arnold Schwarzenegger

That is when I came to your class. Inside a little voice came back: "You can do it." I started to believe again. I started living again. What a gift! I have done more in business in the time I took your class than I had done in six months. Not wanting the momentum to stop, I invested in your Mold Your Mind tape series, and have chosen to retake the class again. I will also be attending the February sessions. I can't wait.

Gary, thank you. Thank you, thank you, thank you. I will debut on stage at a seminar. I will leave my teaching job to pursue my biggest passion – working with people (people who want to be worked with). Until our paths cross again, have a wonderful holiday. God bless you!

Sincerely,
Cyndi D.

I am so humbled by the compliments in Cyndi's letter, and I share them not to show off or to try to convince you that I hold some kind of magic. I have gotten Cyndi's permission to include this letter to show you that if you want to change, learn to be kind to yourself, find some new ways, get some support and be persistent. You can accomplish anything you can imagine. Even when Cyndi seemed so far from her goal, she never gave up, and the results have been fantastic. Some four years later, Cyndi is now a sales director with Mary Kay, and her business and her life continue to improve. You, too, can achieve success. Hang in there. You're worth it.

Finding Your Inner Power

Write out a commitment to yourself and your goal. State clearly for yourself that you will KEEP WATERING, even when it seems you are merely wetting the dirt. Know that establishing that solid root base takes time and that changes are not always immediately apparent. Write it out for yourself that you fully intend to do what it takes. Let yourself know you are in it for the long haul. After all, the "it" is a better life for yourself, and YOU are worthy... now!

Also, be prepared for adversity—and determine in advance that hanging in there through thick and thin will reveal your character.

There's a legendary story about the wine-growing region around Bordeaux. Traditionally, growers gather each year and pray for a good crop of grapes so that they will have wine that will sell at a good price. One year when they gathered to pray in a little country chapel, a particular group of vineyard keepers had an experience of hearing a voice coming through the dome of the chapel that said, "I will give you whatever weather you ask for." "This is incredible," they said among themselves. "God is willing to give us whatever weather we request for the grapes. What shall we do?" They developed a calendar of when they wanted rain, when they wanted sun, when they wanted a lower temperature, a little higher temperature, and they had it all calibrated, and they said, "If God will give us all of this, we will have the best crop of grapes imaginable, and we'll be fabulously successful."

Be prepared for adversity—and determine in advance that hanging in there through thick and thin will reveal your character.

So, they laid it out and presented it to God, and God said, "Agreed, I understand." As the seasons moved along, day by day the weather came the way they had programmed it and sketched it out on the calendar—rain when they wanted rain, sun when they asked for sun, and so forth.

At the end of the year they gathered up the grapes for harvest. The grapes were terrible. And they said, "How could this be? What went wrong? God gave us totally what we asked for. We know what will make good grapes. We know the kind of weather that we truly need.... What could have gone wrong?" And God answered them and said, "You forgot to ask for the harsh north wind against which the grapes have to struggle to mature."

Isn't that a wonderful story? It's those winds of adversity that make us strong—if we struggle against them in the right way.

Be persistent. Change takes time. It is the repetition and practice of the everyday steps that create positive change. Forgive yourself for your failures and celebrate your successes.

Notes:

____
____
____
____
____
____
____
____
____
____
____
____
____
____

My successes to date are:

1. ____
2. ____
3. ____
4. ____
5. ____
6. ____
7. ____
8. ____
9. ____
10. ____

My future successes will be:

1.____
2.____
3.____
4.____
5.____
6.____
7.____
8.____
9.____
10.____

C H A P T E R   E I G H T

Walking the Talk

Go confidently in the direction of your dreams. Live the life you have imagined.
—Henry David Thoreau

WALK THE WALK! TALK IT! Think it. Believe it as if it were a DONE DEAL! Go back to chapter one and revisit the goals you wrote there. Whatever your goals, see yourself as having already achieved them. Get your seventy-five trillion cells believing that is who you are already. You may have to lie to yourself at first, but know that it's in there. Remember the bad waitress I spoke about earlier? There was a great waitress inside of her waiting to be released. I want you to tap into the greatness that is already inside of you.

Nothing can stop the man with the right mental attitude from achieving his goals; nothing on earth can help the man with the wrong mental attitude.
–W.W. Ziege

Can I interest you in identifying what is inside of you so you can move on to other things in your life? In three minutes I WILL teach you how to break through your limiting beliefs—your ten-inch frying pan, so to speak. You will reach that point and know that you have changed forever. You have already examined why you have fears. You have allowed me to help you take the first steps to finding the power that lives inside you.

At the end of my seminar, I offer participants the opportunity to assign specific goals to a board. They write out goals

Always bear in mind that your own resolution to success is far more important than any other one thing.
–Abraham Lincoln

with dates on a piece of wood, and we symbolically "break through" their fears by breaking the board. After they break a board, they find that their reference point has changed. Their own minds do the "computer search." I do not do this for them.

First, they acknowledge the need; second, they examine why they have fears—wood might hurt. By step five they allow themselves to learn new ways. During the seminar they find a support system as the crowd yells a resounding "YES!" for their efforts. They find themselves at step seven and don't quit. They think it, walk it, talk it, and in the end, find it is a done deal.

The board is a metaphor. It represents all the fears we carry around with us. There's a bit of humor in this. Our fear can get so strong that it immobilizes us and causes diarrhea. There is one room in the house that turns out to be our favorite, and we never want to leave it: the bathroom. We have to find our own inner power to change and break through that fear if we are to become all we are meant to be.

There are many medical epidemics today, but I think the most damaging epidemic is that which resides in the human spirit in the form of lack of self-confidence. If someone told you that you were not good at something, you may have believed it all your life. We do the greatest damage to ourselves when we allow these fears to morph into beliefs. The good news is, we have the power to step away from the fear whenever we make up our minds to do so.

The following story appears in *Alternative Medicine*, compiled by the Zurion Goodbury Group (pp. 306-307). I once knew a young man who had a job as a construction worker. He was taking down a wooden frame into which cement had been poured. A nail punctured the bottom of his foot and came out the top of his foot. Although he was bleeding and in terrible pain, his supervisor wouldn't let him seek medical treatment. By the time he worked all day on the injured foot and got to the doctor, his foot had been so badly damaged that he was not able to work for the next three years. He couldn't put any weight on his foot, and his leg was always cold. It was a year and a half before they were able to determine that he had reflex sympathetic dystrophy. For three years, his sister suggested he call a certified hypnotherapist to help him deal with the pain.

At one point he had a thermogram—an x-ray of a part of the body that reveals that part's temperature by different colors. By means of the thermogram, it was easy to determine that the injured foot was eleven degrees colder than a normal foot. After the thermogram the man was told he would certainly be facing amputation, first the toes, then the foot and then the leg. The man wanted the doctor to amputate right away, because the pain was so bad. The doctor spoke with him about phantom pain. Even in instances where limbs have been amputated, the patient often experiences a lingering "memory" of pain that seems as though it is actually occurring at that very moment.

That night, as the man with the abnormally cold foot pondered the information he had been given, he called me and asked whether I thought the human mind could help with his particular condition. My answer was—and remains the same today—"It does not matter what *I* think you can do. It matters what *you* think you can do." That takes me right back to an earlier part in this book when I say, "You can when you believe you can." Or to put it the way Henry Ford did, "You can when you *think* you can."

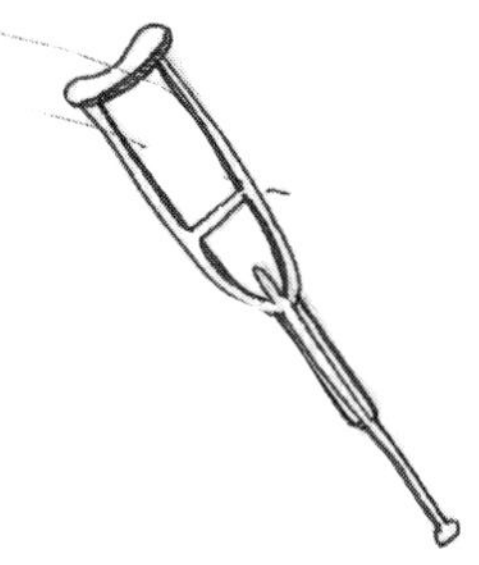

We began work in January, one day a week, one hour each session. In February he told his doctor that he had healed himself and requested another thermogram. The doctor expressed his disbelief, stating that the man's condition was an "incurable" disease. However, at the man's insistence, he was given another thermogram on February 27.

His doctor marveled at the results. The test showed that the injured foot was now only two degrees colder than a normal foot. The doctor wondered how a person could do this. He told the man that he should accept the improvement as "good enough." But the man assured the doctor that he would be back. On July 31, 1991, he had a third thermogram, which showed that both feet were now at the same temperature. I met the man again in 2002, although in a sorrowful circumstance—his mother's funeral—and he was still enjoying complete recovery from an "incurable" disease.

In the end, the quality of your life depends on the quality of your thoughts.

In the end, the quality of your life depends on the quality of your thoughts. Get involved. Check your thinking. If you get anything out of this book, please take this with you. You talk to yourself more than anybody else does. There's a voice that runs a near-constant monologue inside you. I'm asking you to begin listening to that voice. How many times does it say, "Way to go!"? "Nice job!"? Fully realize within yourself that there is much power in that voice.

For a long time it was thought that we heard through sound. In fact, we hear through vibrations. When I speak to you, it sets off vibrations. Your ears collect the vibrations and shoot a message to the brain based upon these vibrations. If you'd like to experience this for yourself, place your hand on your chest and say out loud, "My name is ___." Could you feel the vibration?

I want you to understand that your body is constantly under the impact of these vibrations. We used to think that only the brain had a memory. We know now that every cell of our bodies has a memory. And as I stated earlier, there are 75 trillion cells in your body. Each of those has a memory. These cells play big roles in who we are. Our bodies are brand new every seven years as the cells die off and replace themselves. One might wonder for a moment, how do these cells keep coming back the same? They pass on the memory of the vibrations that run through you.

You can take instant control of your life if you'll just start taking control of those voices, and their vibrations, in your head.

That is how I moved from being an alcoholic for twenty-five years to being a non-drinker, and I make it very clear that I am a non-drinker—I am not in recovery. I changed the vibrations, I changed the voices, I changed the message, and I came to see myself as I did back in 1987, as a non-drinker—a happy, healthy, successful person. I saw it as a done deal.

Another exercise I do at my seminar demonstrates the power of our thoughts. I use an imaginary solid steel rod, which I "cut" into two pieces. Using the power of suggestion, I "implant" one imaginary steel rod in the arm of a volunteer. The arm "becomes" the steel rod. It will not bend. Next I "implant" an imaginary seven-foot steel rod into the volunteer's spine—again, using the power of suggestion. I tell the volunteer that he or she is a steel rod. Within seconds his or her body is completely rigid and will not bend. The volunteer is easily able to support the weight of a person sitting on his or her body as it bridges two chairs.

Even people with histories of "back problems" experience no tension from this exercise. It is because in their minds they are as steel. The "unbending rod" supports the other volunteer because the person allows himself or herself to believe it is so. This process, again, takes minutes, perhaps even seconds. I did this again recently, and the lady who sat on the volunteer was at least fifty pounds heavier than the lady between the two chairs. The little thin lady whose body had become an "unbending rod" said, "I didn't even know that woman was sitting on me."

How can you use this illustration to its maximum potential? When you want to make a sale, do you want to walk into a prospect's office believing he has already bought from you, or believing he won't buy? If a man can convince himself in thirty seconds that he's a solid steel rod, how successful could he be if he convinced himself that he was the greatest salesman in the world? How long will it take you to talk yourself into success? How long will it take you to talk yourself into believing you are worthy? How long will it take you to believe that you are the number-one salesperson, or the best spouse, or the best parent? We know that it takes twenty-one days to form a new habit. It took the volunteers less than thirty seconds to talk themselves into being a piece of steel.

By helping people tap into their unconscious minds, I have had success in working with people with diabetes. I usually ask people what happened six months to two years before their diagnosis; many times there had been a death, divorce or job loss. Literally all the sweetness had gone out of their lives. They formed a belief deep within their minds that life was no longer a sweet place to be. Their bodies then reacted with the condition we call sugar diabetes.

If we can make ourselves ill, I believe we can also make ourselves well. All I'm asking you to do is to understand more and more that you have the most awesome power inside you. Talk to yourself, talk to yourself, talk to yourself—but talk to yourself correctly. The gift is inside you. The greatness is inside you. What a wonderful empowerment it can be when you allow yourself to fully realize that!

It's perhaps the most important thing you can understand when you realize that it is you alone who has the ability to make a profound impact on your life. It is through the power of your own belief that you can tap into exactly what you need to change your life forever. Realize that the past is just that—the past. You did the best you could with the information you had at the time. Then, allow yourself to move forward into your future, away from the past. Know it's a done deal! When you believe you can, you WILL. You will know your dreams because you live them.

Within each waking moment we take steps. It is entirely within our power to choose to make those steps with a true purpose or to merely continue wandering blindly. We choose. We may choose through active involvement, or we may simply choose by unconsciously refusing to plan. Either way, the course of our lives is formed by our thoughts. We can choose to remain powerless. We can choose to retain the appearance of walking onward, even while we know our feet are simply falling into the prints we've traveled before. Or, we can decide today that the path we've been traveling on is getting us nowhere. Decide today that the comfort zone is no longer especially comfortable. Choose to step out of it and into the life that has been waiting for you all along! Choose to use the power you have living inside you—the power to change.

It is through the power of your own belief that you can tap into exactly what you need to change your life forever.... When you believe you can, you WILL. You will know your dreams because you live them.

Harnessing the Power to Change

This exercise demonstrates dramatically how each of us possesses the power to change. As I have mentioned before, the human central nervous system does not differentiate between illusion and reality. What we tell ourselves is exactly what our body believes we're supposed to do. This is a little three-part exercise that we can do all by ourselves on a weekly, monthly, or yearly basis to continue to expand our perceptions of our world.

Part One: Stand in the middle of a room where you have at least a three- or four-foot clearance all around you. Stand with your feet side-by-side with the heels touching, and get balanced and comfortable in that position. If you're right-handed, use your right hand. If you're left-handed, use your left hand. Raise your arm in front of you, make a fist, and point. It's important to remain standing in the same spot for the duration of this short exercise, with your right hand extended, your feet in the same place. Remaining perfectly balanced, turn your upper body slowly to the right if you're right-handed, or to the left if you're left-handed, until you can move no further. Stare down your arm and make a mental note of what your index finger is pointing at. Now bring your arm all the way around to the front again and drop it to your side. Stay in place.

Part Two: Locate a spot that is twelve or fifteen inches further than your initial stopping point, and make a mental note of this new spot. Remember, your feet are in the same position. With this new spot on the screen of your imagination, take a deep breath, let it out, close your eyes and resume breathing normally. Don't move a muscle. We do Part Two all on the screen of our imagination.

Nothing contributes so much to tranquilizing the mind as a steady purpose–a point on which the soul may fix its intellectual eye.
–Mary Shelley

With your eyes closed, breathing normally, see, imagine, and pretend your arm coming up, making a fist and pointing, just like before. Without moving a muscle, remain in balance. See, imagine, and pretend yourself turning as you did before. See, imagine, and pretend yourself turning past all the spots you turned past before. There's your original stopping point. Keep going until you see your new stopping spot. That's the one twelve or fifteen inches past your first stopping spot. Once you can see, imagine, and pretend that you have achieved your new stopping point, give yourself a little smile and begin to unwind. Turn back to your original position, and let your hand drop to your side. Remember, part two of this exercise you did only on the screen of your imagination.

Part Three: To prove to yourself that the central human nervous system does not differentiate between illusion and reality, open your eyes. Bring your hand up in front of you again. Make a fist and point. This time, turn to your new goal or beyond. In most cases, you'll go not only beyond your first stopping point but also your second goal.

We set such limiting beliefs about ourselves all the time. We live within such tight parameters. If you can change the parameters, you can accomplish whatever you dream. I ask people to keep repeating this because it helps us continue to expand our horizons. Our life is a done deal, based on the messages we send ourselves. You can change your life by changing the messages you send yourself. These messages can cause you to continually break through and experience the true power to change.

That's a powerful little exercise. And it doesn't matter if the person is eight or eighty. Every time they've done it they say, "Wow, I didn't think I could do that."

But, in fact, they did accomplish it. And I go back to them and I say, "Now that you know that you did that which you didn't think you could do, what else can you get done that you have previously felt you couldn't do?"

Finding Your Inner Power

Stand tall and walk the talk. Your body hears every word you say. So as you set out on your new journey, you must think it, believe it, talk it, and walk it. Your positive changes are "a done deal!"

Notes:

____
____
____
____
____
____
____
____
____
____
____
____
____
____

The best things I say to myself are:

1.____
2.____
3.____
4.____
5.____
6.____
7.____
8.____
9.____
10.____

C H A P T E R   N I N E

Enjoying Your New Life

But if you have nothing at all to create, perhaps you create yourself.
—Carl Jung

IF YOU HAVE ABSORBED THE LESSONS thus far in the book, you have reached a different place. You have an "inner knowing," a new peace, more joy. Rather than that mode of constant searching, wandering and wondering, "Why am I here?" "What is my purpose?" "What am I going to do with the rest of my life?" you've begun to experience a daily assurance of your worth and your role in the universe.

Life will continue to "get in your way." There will be surprises, challenges. Call them "opportunities," if you will. Some will be positive, some will be negative. They're all part of the journey. Yes, people around you will still become sick. You or family members or friends will have car accidents. Someone may sue you. Loved ones will die. But as you move through all these things, you will be buoyed up by a greater sense of peace and a knowledge that whatever happens, you'll be able to cope. You have found your equilibrium, your center, and you can hold onto it.

The steps you have learned here, however, are not meant only as a linear progression. They are cyclical. Just as members of a twelve-step program such as AA or Al-Anon derive much comfort and support from going back through the steps of their spiritual journey, so, too, will you be helped by reviewing and even repeating the steps in this program. The "ninth step," in fact, is your new life itself, based on heightened awareness, better self-love, additional support from friends, and a desire to maintain and deepen what you have achieved.

I can measure how far I have come in my own journey by thinking back to the occasion of my first opportunity to speak before a business group. Up to that point I had been doing one-on-one coaching, and had gotten into a comfort zone with it. Then a lady offered me the chance to present in front of a group—my first professional speaking engagement! Like I said before, I asked the dry cleaner to starch my pants stiff so that people couldn't see my legs shaking. I was just that insecure, just that uncertain that what I had to say would be perceived as worthwhile.

The "ninth step," in fact, is your new life itself, based on heightened awareness, better self-love, additional support from friends, and a desire to maintain and deepen what you have achieved.

Here's a great story about one of my workshop attendees who moved to a much higher place of consciousness. Her name was Veronica Edwards, and she was part of a brand new class at a Ford Motor Company facility. The class was to run for nine weeks, two hours each week. One session built on the next. Well, Veronica arrived at the class with wrist supports on both hands. I looked at her and said, "Oh my, what's going on here? Are you wearing those as costume jewelry?"

And she said, "This is supposed to be a support class, not a humor class. I have carpal tunnel syndrome. It's obvious to me that you've never had it, because if you had, you would know that the pain it causes is why I wear these."

By this time she was hot under the collar. Nonetheless, I plowed ahead. "I have another question for you," I said. "What do you feel you're gaining by having carpal tunnel syndrome?"

She stood up and came very close to me and said, "Do you want to repeat that question?" Now Veronica Edwards was strong enough that I knew my physical being was in danger. But I did repeat the question anyway. At that point I got very fortunate. Veronica spun around and left the room. And when she closed the door behind her, there was probably not a single person in the entire building that did not hear that door being slammed shut. I didn't know if I would ever see her again. Or what she might do to me if I did.

The following week I arrived in the training room early, and there was Veronica, standing there with her hands on her hips. She said, "Oh, they let you back in, did they?" Here comes trouble, I thought to myself. Veronica, however, surprised me. "I've thought all week about your question, you know, about what did I have to gain by having carpal tunnel," she said. "I'm scared that you might know something that I don't know. So I've decided I'm going to listen in on your class, just in case you might have some important insight for me."

Things changed rapidly between Veronica and me from that point on. She started asking questions in class, questions about awareness. "Where are we?" The answer was simply, "Here." "What time is it?" The answer was simply, "Now." She began to understand the bit about how we live 95 percent of our lives on automatic pilot, and miss so much of the vital awareness of the "here" and the "now." Veronica showed up early for each class, she stayed in the room during the breaks, she stayed after class. She couldn't get enough of asking me questions and chewing on the answers.

The fifth week's class time came, and no Veronica. By now I had really been looking forward to seeing her. I was heartbroken. As I was moving along doing the class, the Ford executive in charge of overseeing their training courses comes charging through the door and said, "Gary, there's a lady outside who would like to see you, and see you NOW."

I said, "Well, I'm in the middle of an exercise here; I'll catch her at break time."

He said, "You need to see her now!" Since this gentleman was controlling my income at the time, I left the classroom and went outside. There was Veronica Edwards standing there, her hands up in the air, tears streaming down her face. And she was saying, "They're gone, they're gone!" And sure enough, her wrists were bare -- no more supports.

"What happened?" I asked, stunned.

"I just came from the Ford doctors, Gary. I told them, 'Please take these supports off, because I won't need them anymore.'" She gave them to me and said, "Maybe they can be a help to somebody else."

I was worried that she might have acted too precipitously. "Veronica," I said, "why don't you need the supports anymore?"

To be what we are, and to become what we are capable of becoming, is the only end of life.
–Robert Louis Stevenson

"Get a load of this," she replied. "I found out why I needed them. I got laid off from Ford when I was just three years into this job. I was laid off for five years. I'm a single mother raising a teenager. So what did I do? I waited tables, I cleaned houses, I did whatever I had to in order to keep her in clothes, send her to school, buy her books, feed her. When Ford called me back, I came to believe that what I needed was to have a disability, because the company rule is that nobody can get laid off when they're on medical restrictions."

I found out that that was not actually a true statement. It didn't matter, because Veronica had believed it was true, and had acted accordingly. In her new consciousness she was no longer afraid of being laid off again by Ford. She knew she had the strength to cope and make her way through life, with Ford or without Ford.

Interestingly, I carry those wrist supports with me to many of my workshops. I look at the people and I say, "You know, I don't know what you're here for and I don't know what you want to gain from it, but let me show you what one person did gain from this workshop." And I tell the story about Veronica Edwards.

Some of us let years go by before the awareness of how we are loved and appreciated dawns on us. I know I did. There was a time when I would have opted for cremation instead of a funeral with a cemetery burial, because I was sure there weren't six people willing to serve as pallbearers for me.

There's a story that comes from *Chicken Soup® for the Teenage Soul* that really touched me. It was a tradition in this particular family that when a son graduated from high school, he received a brand new car as a gift. So for three weeks before graduation, father and son went looking for the perfect car. They kicked scores of tires, they test drove dozens of vehicles, they listened to car radios and checked colors and designs, until finally they found the perfect car. Imagine the son's excitement when, upon his graduation, his father presented him with a gift-wrapped box. The son opened the box to discover a copy of the Holy Bible. With despair and anger he returned the Bible to his father and ranted, "Thank you for the disappointment. I will never speak to you again as long as I live." And he stormed out of the house.

Years later the son got a phone call from his mother announcing that his father had died. The son came home for the funeral, and after the service he was going through many of his dad's possessions, the ones that had been set aside for him in the inheritance. When he came upon the Bible his father had given him as a graduation gift, he wiped the dust from the cover and opened it. The Bible fell open to a certified check stuck in between two pages, dated the day of his graduation, for the exact amount of that special car.

The gift is already inside of you. You have to open your book and find it. Nobody else but you is going to be turning the pages of your life. So, day by day, get involved in discovering your greatness. There's so much there of worth, a whole treasure.

And how are you doing on your commitment to give compliments? Do you remember what the average number of compliments is for human beings in our society? Did you say "one a week"? That's pretty far off. It's actually one a month. I have asked you to improve upon that average.

Day by day, get involved in discovering your greatness. There's so much there of worth, a whole treasure.

Are you giving at least five compliments a day by now? That's good. Now I'd like you to raise that number to ten. That's correct: ten compliments a day. You'll be amazed at how it will come back to you. And thank people for who they are and what they have done for you and others. Saying thanks, in the right way, can also double as a compliment.

Early on in this book I mentioned goal-setting. It's so important. Now that you have been through the steps, you are ready to appreciate that importance. To reinforce that notion I'd like to tell you about the experience of a service manager at the Al Dietrich Oldsmobile dealership in Waterford, Michigan. I had great respect for Al and his dealership, and I was always driving an Olds I had bought from him and relying upon the service department to keep my cars in tip-top shape.

One day I called for a service appointment, and the manager said, "Hey, strange that you should call. A letter you mailed to me arrived at our house yesterday. My wife calls me at work about it and says, 'When did you start writing letters to yourself?' After twenty years of marriage she knew my handwriting cold. 'What's going on here?' she asks me.

"I told her I'd look at the letter when I got home tonight. When I got home I immediately realized the envelope was the one I addressed to myself in your workshop. Remember? You told us to write out our 101 goals, make you a copy and turn them in, and you would mail the list back to us in a year. Well, Gary, I didn't have 101 goals; I came up with only twenty-two. I didn't photocopy my goals, either. I just tore the page out of the workbook, folded it up, put it in an envelope, and gave it to you. I just wanted to get you off my back. Do you know what, though?

A year later, of those twenty-two goals I'd put down, I'd accomplished eleven."

This story shows you the power of writing your goals down. Even though that service manager did not keep a copy and had nothing to look at over that year, the act of writing down his goals on paper, I believe, also inscribed them in his mind. And his mind saw to it that he carried out eleven of the twenty-two.

Close your eyes and picture yourself as the success that God, you, and your family want you to be. Be specific. If you're in sales, see your next quarter's totals up sharply from the previous quarter. If you're an employee, see yourself as a highly regarded producer at work, someone your boss and your peers admire and respect. If you're a spouse at home keeping the nest, get a vision of a household transformed by your creativity, love, and positive energy.

True happiness... is not attained through self-gratification but through fidelity to a worthy purpose.
–Helen Keller

Let's resume here our discussion on goal setting. I'd like to add one more example -- something so powerful that I hope it will leave you inspired and determined to go and do likewise.

Mark Victor Hansen was sitting on an airplane, which he does 200 days out of the year, and a flight attendant came up to him and said, "I know *you*. You wrote that book *Dare to Win*—incredible book." Mark acknowledged that he was the author in question and, shortly, other flight attendants began to congregate around his row. So much so that the gentleman sitting next to Mark got up to give them some more room and walked off down the aisle. When the flight attendants went back to their work, this gentleman returned to his seat and said to Mark:

"That was quite a busy activity; what was that all about?"

"I was fortunate enough to write a book called *Dare to Win*, and that lady had read it and enjoyed it."

"What kind of work do you do?" the gentleman asked Mark.

"I help people live their dreams."

"Really? What's your name?"

"Mark Victor Hansen."

"Well, I never heard of you."

So Mark turned to his seatmate and asked, "And who are you, sir?"

For the purposes of this story let's just say the man's name was "Bill Smith."

Mark pursued the conversation, asking, "What sort of work do you do?"

The gentleman responded:

"Well, I'm in the process right now of creating the world's largest shop-at-home network. I'm going to have five GE satellites in space, and within a few years (this was back in the 1990s) you'll be able to buy anything that you want right off that home network."

"Wow!" Mark said. "That must have taken some planning."

"You'd better believe it," the man replied. "And you, since you help people live their dreams, you must talk to them about goal setting."

"Absolutely," Mark admitted. "I teach everybody to write out 101 goals."

"Only 101?" Bill Smith came back. "Then you must be relatively new to this goal-setting stuff. I have over 500."

Then Mark got bold and asked to see Mr. Smith's goals.

Like Mark Victor Hansen, Mr. Smith carried his goals with him all the time. A bit reluctantly, he pulled the sheets containing his goals from the breast pocket of his jacket and handed them to Mark.

Mark opened the sheets and began reading. Shortly, he took a pen from his pocket and put a line through one of Mr. Smith's goals, and wrote his initials next to it. Then he did the same for two or three more goals.

"What are you doing to my goals?" Mr. Smith broke in.

"Hang on," said Mark as he lined through still more goals and initialed them. "Here's my business card. I'll be back in my office Monday. Call me and I'll introduce you to people who can help you fulfill each of the goals I've lined through."

There's an interesting follow-up to this story. "Bill Smith" needed a half-billion dollars of venture capital to keep his home-shopping project funded through to the finish. Two or three weeks later, Mark Victor Hansen, on another of his 200 airplane trips per year, was sitting next to a gentleman from Asia who represented a group of investors looking to plow $10 billion into a variety of ventures around the world. So Mark hooked the Asian gentleman up with Bill Smith's company—and, of course, later received a generous referral fee.

Life is for the dreamers and the doers. Be both. Your accomplishments will be many, your regrets will be few, and your cup will overflow with satisfaction and joy.

What would it take for you to sit down right now or the coming weekend and write out 101 goals for your life? That's the challenge as you finish this book. Once you've got them down on paper, prioritize them. And as you find yourself accomplishing a goal, cross it off, date it, and replace it with a new one.

Life is for the dreamers and the doers. Be both. Your accomplishments will be many, your regrets will be few, and your cup will overflow with satisfaction and joy.

Finding Your Inner Power

No longer are you living your life by the negative opinions of others, nor by your own negative opinions. You are now an enthusiastic goal-setter and achiever. Your life is on an upward curve toward new and exciting heights!

Here are some books to support you in your power to change:

Your Body Believes Every Word You Say, by Barbara Hoberman Levine (WordsWork Press, 2000)

From a Chicken to an Eagle, by Jerry Frankhauser (Frankhauser, 1982)

The Choice, by Og Mandino (Bantam, 1986)

What to Say When You Talk to Yourself, by Shad Helmstetter (MJF Books, 1997; Pocket, 1990)

Feel the Fear and Do It Anyway, by Susan Jeffers (Ballantine, 1988)

Notes:

Put your goals in writing. Putting a goal down on paper multiplies, by several times, the likelihood of your achieving it. Aim for 101 goals. If you find you have more than that, attach a sheet and paste or staple it into this book.

1. ____
2. ____
3. ____
4. ____
5. ____
6. ____
7. ____
8. ____
9. ____
10. _______________________________________
11. _______________________________________
12. _______________________________________
13. _______________________________________
14. _______________________________________
15. _______________________________________
16. _______________________________________
17. _______________________________________
18. _______________________________________
19. _______________________________________
20. _______________________________________
21. _______________________________________
22. _______________________________________
23. _______________________________________
24. _______________________________________
25. _______________________________________
26. _______________________________________

27. ____________________
28. ____________________
29. ____________________
30. ____________________
31. ____________________
32. ____________________
33. ____________________
34. ____________________
35. ____________________
36. ____________________
37. ____________________
38. ____________________
39. ____________________
40. ____________________
41. ____________________
42. ____________________
43. ____________________
44. ____________________
45. ____________________
46. ____________________
47. ____________________
48. ____________________
49. ____________________
50. ____________________
51. ____________________
52. ____________________
53. ____________________
54. ____________________
55. ____________________
56. ____________________
57. ____________________

58. ______
59. ______
60. ______
61. ______
62. ______
63. ______
64. ______
65. ______
66. ______
67. ______
68. ______
69. ______
70. ______
71. ______
72. ______
73. ______
74. ______
75. ______
76. ______
77. ______
78. ______
79. ______
80. ______
81. ______
82. ______
83. ______
84. ______
85. ______
86. ______
87. ______
88. ______

All our dreams can come true–if we have the courage to pursue them.
–Walt Disney

89. ______________________________
90. ______________________________
91. ______________________________
92. ______________________________
93. ______________________________
94. ______________________________
95. ______________________________
96. ______________________________
97. ______________________________
98. ______________________________
99. ______________________________
100. ______________________________
101. ______________________________

About Gary Lalonde

Gary Lalonde is a unique helper who has broken through to a world where few folks travel.

He has seen the illusion of suffering and fear and loneliness. All of these experiences he manifested in alcoholism and illness.

For many years his teachings as a keynote presenter and as a trainer all center on the universal truth: There must be and there is a way out of the human problem, and any enlightened person can find it.

Your journey of enlightenment will open you to a life of unbelievable discoveries.

For further information or to arrange a personal appearance, contact Gary at gary@garylalonde.com or telephone him at 800-577-U-CAN.

ADDITIONAL EMPOWERMENT TOOLS BY GARY LALONDE

VIDEO SERIES: The entire five sessions of RELEASING THE POWER WITHIN learning experience on VHS Casssettes, including workbook.

The 8 Steps to Change
Self-talk & Affirmations
Understanding & Setting Goals
3 Channels of Communications
Save the Feelings

Videos also available separately.

AUDIO:

Subliminal learning program #1 WEIGHT LOSS
Subliminal learning program #2 STOP SMOKING
Subliminal learning program #5 BEST IN YOU
Subliminal learning program #7 OVERCOMING FEAR & WORRY
Subliminal learning program #14 STOP PROCRASTINATING
Subliminal learning program #16 THINK YOURSELF TO GREATER RICHES
Subliminal learning program #17 SALES PROGRAM FOR SALESPEOPLE
Subliminal learning program #30 SELF-CONFIDENCE
Subliminal learning program #31 ELEVATE YOUR SELF-IMAGE
Subliminal learning program #33 POWER OF POSITIVE THINKING

For assistance with your selection, contact us at www.garylalonde.com.